Crassus

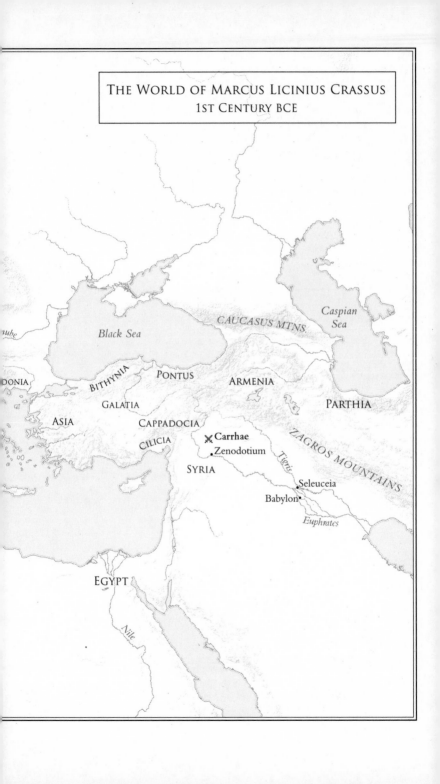

THE WORLD OF MARCUS LICINIUS CRASSUS
1ST CENTURY BCE

Caspian Sea

CAUCASUS MTNS.

Black Sea

DONIA

BITHYNIA

PONTUS

ARMENIA

PARTHIA

GALATIA

ASIA

CAPPADOCIA

ZAGROS MOUNTAINS

CILICIA

✗ **Carrhae**

• Zenodotium

Tigris

SYRIA

• Seleuceia

Babylon •

Euphrates

EGYPT

Nile

Crassus

The First Tycoon

Peter Stothard

· ANCIENT LIVES ·

Yale

UNIVERSITY PRESS

NEW HAVEN & LONDON

Published with assistance from the foundation established in memory of
Amasa Stone Mather of the Class of 1907, Yale College.

Yale University Press books may be purchased in quantity for
educational, business, or promotional use. For information, please e-mail
sales.press@yale.edu (U.S. office) or sales@yaleup.co.uk (U.K. office).

Set in the Yale typeface designed by Matthew Carter, and Louize,
designed by Matthieu Cortat, by Integrated Publishing Solutions.
Printed in Great Britain by TJ Books Ltd, Padstow, Cornwall.

Frontispiece: Beehive Mapping.

Library of Congress Control Number: 2022931861
ISBN 978-0-300-25660-4 (hardcover : alk. paper)

A catalogue record for this book is available from the British Library.

10 9 8 7 6 5 4 3 2

MIX
Paper from
responsible sources
FSC
www.fsc.org   FSC® C013056

· ANCIENT LIVES ·

Ancient Lives unfolds the stories of thinkers, writers, kings, queens, conquerors, and politicians from all parts of the ancient world. Readers will come to know these figures in fully human dimensions, complete with foibles and flaws, and will see that the issues they faced—political conflicts, constraints based in gender or race, tensions between the private and public self—have changed very little over the course of millennia.

James Romm
Series Editor

To Ruth

Contents

Contents

Crassus

Prologue

The first tycoon of ancient Rome was also its most famous loser. If Marcus Licinius Crassus had died in 54 BCE he might have quietly entered history as Rome's richest man, its first modern financier and political fixer, the brutal victor in a war against escaped slaves and an equal of Julius Caesar, whom he had played a huge part in creating. His modern face would have been from 1960, Laurence Olivier in Stanley Kubrick's *Spartacus*. Instead, late in life, Crassus led an army on an unprovoked campaign against Parthia into what are now the borderlands of Turkey, Syria, and Iraq. He lost a desert battle and the eagle standards of his legions near a small town called Carrhae. His head became a stage prop in a Greek tragedy in a city that the Romans saw as too barbarian for such entertainment. Storytellers described his dead mouth stuffed with gold. The legacy of Crassus was a peculiarly catastrophic defeat that took a potent hold on the Roman mind. Thirty years later the emperor Augustus judged the return of Crassus's eagles as among his greatest achievements, worthy to be recorded by his greatest poets and sculptors. Crassus was no ordinary failure, just as he had been no ordinary success — a man whose life as business-man and politician posed both immediate and lasting questions about the intertwining of money, ambition, and power.

CHAPTER ONE

The Secret Disrupter

Marcus Licinius Crassus was in his early sixties in the summer of 54 BCE, fit but old for a Roman army commander, red-cloaked and almost ready to cross the Euphrates for an unprecedented eastern war. Crassus was a meticulous planner, a master of political and financial risk. In these hottest months before the invasion he was making detail the servant of his grand design, just as he had all his life: the heavy equipment of his men, their means of supply, the guides that he needed for where later commanders would have maps. His war was to be waged at the edges of what he or any Roman properly knew. Before his seven legions could advance against Parthia's King of Kings, extending Rome's dominion through the deserts to China, there were humdrum administrative and financial tasks ahead, the kind for which he was already renowned.

Crassus was a Roman who rarely traveled out of Rome, and abroad hardly at all. He owned vast lands in Italy, but unlike other rich Romans, he rarely visited them or drew on them for pleasure or support. His home was Rome, and at different times, he had owned most of its three square miles, selling mansions for the rich and tenement blocks for the poor, lending to those who, unlike himself, wanted more than a single family house, those many Roman politicians with a reach beyond their grasp. He had long been renowned as his city's richest man, its secret financier, disrupter of old rules, fixer and puller of the puppet strings of power. This campaign was meant to mark a change in how men saw him. It was to be Crassus's most public act since his defeat of Spartacus more than fifteen years before, as well as Rome's farthest move into the East in its two hundred years as an empire.

Crassus was not a novice on the battlefield. In what now seemed the distant past, 82 BCE, in his early thirties under the very walls of Rome, he had won a victory that had brought to power the city's first dictator, Lucius Cornelius Sulla. In his forties, he had defeated a slave army that had not only destroyed thousands of farms, many of them his own, but had terrified the city too. In the opening battles of this latest campaign against the Parthians he had won easy victories. But the strengths of his character stood elsewhere, in the arts of control and coercion, means that, with tact and skill, would remain hidden. He was a very secret disrupter. His method was to bind his friends and enemies, the fundamental business of politics, by means softer than the sword.

As the rival of Rome's "first man," Gnaeus Pompeius, twice his colleague as consul, the city's highest office, he had preferred lines of credit to legions. Pompey was five years younger but in 54 BCE was the leading man of Rome as Crassus had reluctantly to admit. Romans called Pompey "the Great" and "the New Alexander," but only ironically if they were looking for Crassus's favor. As a manager of the fast-rising Julius Caesar, who was fifteen years his junior, Crassus had provided massive loans to buy his man the necessary offices of state; some said that he was almost the manufacturer of

Caesar. As a promoter of himself he had less experience. Only late in life, or "not very early in the morning," as one of the kings along his route had just disrespectfully noted, was he planning to march with fifty thousand men, seven legions with seven of their near sacred legionary eagles, to bring into the empire of Rome the Parthian Empire.

This perhaps too candid king was called Deiotarus, Divine Bull of Galatia, one of many local powers who owed his authority to Rome. But Deiotarus was not wrong in his noting of age and time. That summer Crassus looked even older than he was, his chin like an ax, if we trust the portrait from his family tomb, his nose bent downward in common Roman scorn. He knew his strengths. He knew how legions worked, how to make men responsive to orders, the delicate balance required between too much command and too little. He had adapted best military practice for the cohorts of the enslaved who designed, built, bought, and sold his properties. He knew that every grand design was built on detail; but it was a long time since he had had a grand military design of his own.

He had little knowledge of his Parthian adversary, King Orodes, whose coins in the marketplace suggested a not much younger man than himself, bearded, with a wart on his forehead and a star in front of his eyes. As the summer days passed by, Crassus was expecting an ambassador from the devious Orodes, as he deemed him to be, a new king who, he was told, had murdered his father and imprisoned his brother, Mithridates, in one of his riverside palaces. Mithridates was said to be a man more sympathetic to Rome, but only the naive would claim to be certain of that. Crassus was not naive.

He did not know who the ambassador would be, one of the king's most trusted men or a member of one of the warlord families who claimed the Parthian role of kingmakers. One thing he did know: whenever the ambassadors appeared they would instantly signal their difference from himself. They would look different; they would smell differently from Romans — either from their bad characters or their efforts at perfumed disguise. That was in the very nature of a foreigner. Every Roman knew that. As for how Parthia was ruled, he hardly cared; he was sure it was an inferior way to that of Rome. Crassus's reply would be a formality unless the message was of submission without a fight.

A greater cause of concern was the whereabouts of his son, Publius, who was on his way to the Euphrates from Julius Caesar in Gaul. Before he moved further into his Parthian war, Crassus wanted the presence beside him of Publius, already a war hero, the man of his family whom many at Rome admired more than they admired himself. He had another son, Marcus, not quite so respected, who had only just joined Caesar, too, and was staying there. Publius had recently married a young heiress of the Scipios; Marcus was married not quite so well into the same great family from Rome's history. One son in each great theater of war, both offering hope for new Crassi for the future, was a wise insurance against ill fortune: Crassus was a master of insurance.

For his Parthian campaign Crassus needed the military dash that Publius had shown for Caesar as the "conqueror of Aquitania," the rich, gold-mining area of southwest Gaul: this was an impressive commission for Caesar to have entrusted to so young a man and an even greater success in fighting and diplomacy when he completed it. Most of all he wanted his son's Gallic cavalry, small, fast horses with lightly armed riders, especially necessary to protect his legions from enemy cavalry attack in open desert ground. Publius was bringing a thousand horsemen from Caesar, a return of many past favors from the man on the meteoric rise to the older man who felt that he, too, had much farther to go.

There had been delays. It was risky transporting so critical a military asset by sea. But Crassus could be patient. He was expecting help, too, from the neighboring Armenians, often an enemy of Parthia, but that was hardly a necessity. He could see and buy most of what he needed. On the Roman side of the Euphrates he was still among friends. He could exchange news as well as money for men. Everyone wanted his news.

In the past two years he and Caesar had been more openly equals than in his banker's past, the pair of them publicly allied with Pompey, too. Everyone who mattered in Rome, or to Rome, knew that, whatever the rules, the law, the checks and balances of tradition, nothing important could happen in 54 BCE without the say-so of this Three-Headed-Monster, Pompey, Caesar, Crassus, not always, he hoped, in that order of priority.

Pompey, as much the great general as Crassus was the great financier, had been his rival for thirty years, a conqueror of the Near East whose success Crassus wanted to emulate in the much farther east. Caesar, the third man at this time, was five years into his conquest of Gaul, ever more powerful and popular, a balancing weight between them. Crassus was adroit in managing the political scales, and as soon as he had Publius with Caesar's cavalry beside him, his aim was his own imperial glory, a missing part of himself that had so long seemed to him less necessary for power than the ties of money that he notoriously understood so well. Pompey's claim to be the "New Alexander," the heir to the last conqueror of the East, was twenty years old: how much stronger would his own claim be when he, Marcus Licinius Crassus, was the new hero, writing his victory reports to the Senate from Babylon and Susa, legendary cities that he would make Roman and real.

Negotiations had to come first. The Euphrates separated land that was ruled by Rome from friendly border towns that, like all border towns, might sometimes need to change their friends. Since arriving in the region he had coerced, crushed, and bribed. Parthia was a place of rival old families whose loyalty could, he was sure, be bought and sold. Around it were the countries of rival kings whom Romans had bribed before.

He had every reason for confidence. He already had allies in neighboring states. His son was a proven leader. Others of his friends had sent their own sons. His army was not made of Rome's finest (Caesar and Pompey had laid claim to those), but they were undoubtedly, and increasingly, the army of the Crassi. Those who had fought profitably for Pompey in the past hoped that under a commander with the well-known priorities of Crassus, they might bring home more. The experienced trained the inexperienced, just as they did on Crassus's building sites. All owed their pay and their prospects to a single paymaster.

Crassus was a single-minded man who had made his own way. No one would say that he had come from nothing: that would not be possible until the race to be the first man of Rome had led to there being always a single ruler, one emperor after another, some of them hardly even Romans. Crassus was part of the old world, before Rome's empire had an emperor, but he was following a path to power that was very different from his peers'. He was a disrupter of the normal. He had forged the role of Rome's first tycoon.

His father, Publius, was a Roman aristocrat but his mother, Venuleia, was from an Etruscan family of business. He prided himself on understanding risk. He had found safer forms of chance than soldiery and tighter bonds of allegiance than a general could command. He had lived through dramatic times of revolution and reaction and learned lessons that others had missed.

He carried his father's name but acted as his mother's son. He had been as smart as the best Etruscan trader, but on a massive scale, when buying ruined landholdings from victims of Roman civil war. He was innovative when understanding human capital, which, in the early first century BCE, meant buying and training the smartest of the enslaved to manage the greatest property empire that Romans had ever known. He trusted the city more than the country.

He was not a banker in the way that later men would understand the word. He did not make loans for long periods ahead. His sense of the past, like so many of his time and class, was acute and went as far back as he could think; his sense of the future was only of the future that was near. What lay ahead in his mind were never more than fragmented hopes, fuzzy expectations.

But Crassus did not need to have the skills of future tycoons to be ahead of his time. In order to exercise power through money, he needed only to keep the pieces of the future a little more connected than did his peers, a little more like a jigsaw, a little less like clouds of hot air. Even when camped beside the Euphrates, far from his home, he was still a sophisticated banker for his time, a lender to a deep pool of dependent supporters.

He had once lightly said that no one should be called rich who could not pay for an army from his own income. Some saw that as a vulgar boast, though less so at the time of Spartacus's rebellion, when the Roman treasury lacked funds to fight its own slaves. Many saw the only acceptable wealth to be in great estates; this was a view from the past but potent for those who never saw a change that they liked. Crassus's idea of himself as a rich man was as a trader of loans and debts as well as land and votes. As he stared out at distant deserts, he was a controller, a balancer, with a personal grace that hid his insecurity and a potent ambition, no longer hidden, for recognition, not as Rome's first tycoon, but as its first man in every way.

His son, Publius, would be with him soon. They would be able to discuss the coming campaign. There would be news too of Pompey, who, unusually, was in Rome, attempting to pull strings for once without an army behind him, playing the political game like a Crassus while Crassus aspired to be a Pompey. From his son he would also learn more of a rare failure by his protégé, Caesar, in Britain and his characteristic success in persuading the people of Rome that a catastrophe was a triumph. Caesar was a literary artist as well as a general, another new talent that, like finance, had never been necessary for the great Romans of the past.

Crassus and his son considered themselves men of culture. They were certainly more learned in literature and language than in the geography of the Parthian deserts. They knew something of the Tigris and Euphrates Rivers and of the fertile fields where the Persian Empire of Cyrus the Great had risen and fallen before the Greek conquests of Alexander. They knew that greatness could still be had. They knew names of colorless kings; they saw their bearded faces on coins passed throughout the empire; but they knew little directly about those whom they were preparing to fight. They knew much more from their textbooks of how Cyrus was educated six centuries before, the famed tragedies of the Greeks, their stories of hubris and nemesis, pride and fall.

They knew the work of Aristotle; in his entourage Crassus had his own follower of that preeminent Greek philosopher who had been court professor to Alexander. Aristotle had an argument for everything—from the justification of warfare to the use and abuse of money, from the definition of desert animals and plants to the ideal ways to rule a state. Aristotle disapproved of lending money for profit but approved of protecting civilization by enslaving foreigners. A Roman Aristotelian, such as Alexander Polyhistor, who taught Crassus and his sons, soon learned which books of the great man's works would suit his employer best. Moderation was a virtue; man was a "political animal"; those were the starting points.

In this summer of 54 BCE, as he stared into Parthia, there was no thought of ideas beyond the diplomatic, the financial, and the disciplinary. Crassus was not launching a popular war. He had had to threaten to decimate his troops, to force one in ten to be clubbed to death by their colleagues, if their obedience fell below his demands. He had carried out just such a threat once before. He could be a hard man, as everyone knew, also one of the most emollient.

Crassus's legions hoped for quick and well-organized plunder. They knew that they had no one in command like Pompey or Caesar. It had been twenty years since their leader had last led men in action. In 73 BCE Crassus had crushed the Spartacus slave revolt when other commanders had failed. He had crucified thousands of survivors and successfully discouraged any repetition of an outrage to Roman life. The morality of such a horror was no more an issue then than it would have been for Aristotle, but it had not made him a military hero. The humiliation of men bought and sold, once the danger of their liberation was safely past, had not been deemed much of a triumph, certainly not worthy of a march-by triumph through Rome. And to Crassus's powerless disappointment, Pompey had managed to mop up bands of escapers and share the little glory there had been.

Crassus could hope that after the conquest of Parthia, there would be generous prizes for his troops. Pompey had once made the mistake of being mean in the sharing of eastern treasure; it was not a mistake the "great man" had ever made again. After any level of generosity, there would still be massive rewards for Crassus himself and Publius, gold and silver coin and plate, the traditional wealth of conquerors, a different kind from his books of loans and debts, more public, the assets of the kind of leader that he wished to become.

Publius was a loyal as well as scholarly son. He had won high praise not only from Caesar but from the politician and philosopher Marcus Tullius Cicero, who was regularly at odds with Crassus himself. If Publius was discreetly admired more than his father that was to the father's credit — and the mother's, too. They were a close family, loyal to one another. Tertulla had been married first to Crassus's brother, an early victim of Rome's civil wars. The Crassi had lost multiple victims to political murder.

Crassus's marriage then to his brother's widow was in the best tradition of noble family acts, as thirty years before everyone had agreed, but it was no special virtue. Some said that its motive was mainly to avoid returning Tertulla's dowry to her father. That was a common charge against him. Avarice adhered to his reputation like a leech on skin. Much that Crassus did was for money, but everything that he did was interpreted as done for money.

Tertulla, like himself, had to endure aspersions against her good name; some said that in difficult times she had preferred a Sabine man called Quintus Axius to her husband and that their sons showed some proof of this. Crassus's hope was that, after the shared success of Publius and himself against the warlords of the Parthian desert, barbarians with new imperial ambitions dangerously like those of Rome, everything would look different. The family past would be different as well as its future.

As a conqueror in the East, Crassus would have emulated Pompey and Caesar, even the exploits of Cyrus and Alexander — or be able to pretend so. He would leave his sons even richer. There would be money as well as glory to be had, golden thrones to melt down to coins, pillage for his business partners and backers, those who were never far from his thoughts even as his aspirations rose. There was wealth to be gained in Parthia, but even more important than that vital blood of power, there was unconquered power itself.

CHAPTER TWO

A Faraway Place

In the years around 115 BCE, when Marcus Licinius Crassus was born, few Romans thought of Parthia and few Parthians were concentrating on Rome. Both societies were on the outer edges of an ancient world whose cultural center was Greece and would remain so for a century.

Parthians knew Greece. They had fought with the Persians in their fifth-century invasions of Greece. When the Macedonian Greeks fought in Persia after the death of Alexander the Great, there were Parthians on both sides, valued for their archers on horseback. The name of the Parthian king Arsaces was in Aeschylus's play *The Persians,* the first historical tragedy of a failed invasion. Parthians mixed Greek words into their language and watched Greek tragedies and comedies at their courts. Romans did the same, concentrating mostly on the comedies.

In the houses of the great Roman families Parthia was a faraway idea, far from a Rome where military minds were fixed on the threat from the south and north. In the nearer east there were squabbling kings, occasional opportunities for plunder, but even there, no dangers to Rome. Inasmuch as anyone cared about Parthia it was to disparage its people by comparison with Alexander's Greek successors whom they had displaced: "Macedonians had degenerated into Syrians and Parthians," according to a consul at the time.

Parthia was a sprawling country with no clear borders and many capitals. It lay beneath the Black, Caspian, and Aral Seas, from east of the Euphrates through what would become Iraq, Iran, and parts of Pakistan. The Parthi, in their own language, called themselves the exiles. They had come from the North, first as settlers, later as invaders. Two hundred years earlier they had conquered the frail remnants left by Rome's defeat of Alexander's Seleucid successors. The main threat to their security was still from their original northern homeland. Their main opportunities for profit from trade were even farther east.

By 106 BCE their latest possession was the Silk Road city of Merv, where they received embassies from China. Camels laden with silk arrived in Parthia to exchange the world's costliest product for its finest cavalry horses. King Mithridates II, newly styled "king of kings," shown on his coins with a wart under his left eye, a hooked nose, and a square beard, had pushed back northern invaders. He had not yet moved south to the Euphrates. His domain was at peace, and events in Rome were no disturbance to him.

The far east was equally low on the Roman agenda. When Arsaces the Scythian, founder of Parthia's royal family, had led forces down from the Caspian, Roman minds were fixed on the threat from the south, from Carthage in Africa. By the time of Crassus's childhood, when Mithridates was consolidating his control, the Roman army was looking north, to the threat from invaders from Germany, driven south into Italy by flood and famine. After the defeat of Carthage there were new storms at Rome from the south, the massive bribes being offered from King Jugurtha for votes that he might keep his kingdom in Africa.

A scholarly few might have read the *Parthica,* by Apollodorus of Artemita, a Greek writer who lived in what had become the Parthian Empire. But there was never a Parthian population at Rome, none of the guides to understanding, or even prejudiced misunderstanding, that the Romans had for Greeks, Africans, and Gauls.

Eastern affairs were exotic. In Rome there were more pressing concerns, rising claims for citizen rights and redistribution of wealth and land. There was much to discuss about whether two of the Vestal Virgins, keepers of the city's sacred fire, were still virgins and what should be the punishment if they had broken their vows and were not. There was the imminent marriage of Gaius Marius, the top Roman general, who had risen from nowhere, to the aristocrat daughter of Gaius Julius Caesar, who claimed descent from Rome's fourth king. Marius, despite the obscurity of his family, had been the savior of the city in its northern and southern trials, so his wedding to a Caesar was a social matter but not merely social. And then there was the fire of 111 BCE — or 643 AUC, the year calculated *ab urbe condita,* from the city's first foundation — a destruction that marked minds like none would until the reign of Nero.

Crassus's family, one of those that had strengthened its hold on Rome since the defeat of Carthage, looked to the North and West, just as did their peers. When Crassus was eighteen, his father, Publius, was governor of Spain and the author of a pioneer book on the farthest northwest that the Romans recognized, the Tin Islands, sources of an essential metal for armaments, possibly part of Devon and Cornwall or in the estuary of the Loire. Crassus assisted his father in Spain, whose merchants were as secretive about the origins of tin as eastern traders were of how silk was made. The Crassi knew much more about metals than luxury dress materials.

Not until Crassus was in his twenties was there the first official meeting between Romans and Parthians. Lucius Cornelius Sulla, a general campaigning in Cappadocia, met an ambassador from Mithridates II beside the Euphrates. The Parthians inquired about "friendship and alliance," but Sulla thought this beneath consideration. He did not give the Parthian ambassador a private audience. He sat like a judge between him and a minor local king, an act that Mithridates deemed a personal insult, executing his ambassador to prove the point before both sides returned to their mutual unconcern.

CHAPTER THREE

Nothing to Laugh About

Crassus's last sight of his father was of a severed head on a ship's prow in the Forum, one of those on the Rostra, from which Roman politicians made their speeches to the people below. The prows were wooden trophies of a naval war two hundred years before. The enemy then were nearby towns who feared Rome's growing dominance over central Italy: Crassus's father's head was the trophy of what was a continuing war within Italy from south to north, including Rome itself, over rights, privileges, and votes — and it was not the only rotting skull. Eyes of other senators deemed opponents of the dictatorial populist Gaius Marius stared out over the city's political and religious center, some leftward over the sacred fire of Vesta to the moneylenders' booths beneath the Temple of Castor and Pollux, others to the right to the Tabularium, the city treasury, and the Temple of Concord, built to celebrate peace between patricians and the people three hundred years before and needing reinauguration several times since then.

Only weeks before, Crassus's father had been speaking from the Rostra rather than rising from it on a spike. He had a secure place in old Rome, and he hoped to have one in the new. He recognized the need for change. He was no old reactionary. He recognized that the powers expressed in the initials SPQR, Senatus Populusque Romanus, the Senate and the People of Rome, did not need to be in fixed proportions. Rome had long been a rare ancient city ruled by its people, less rare in allowing the landed rich to do the ruling for the landless poor. But the relationship of rich and poor, soldier and civilian, Roman and non-Roman had changed in various ways over the years. It could change again. In flexibility was strength.

Now the views of Publius Crassus no longer mattered except to his son. The Marians alone held the reins of change. This was only partly a triumph of policy; mostly it was the triumph of a man. It was hard for those humiliating their enemies to control where a dead gaze fell, whether a dead mouth was open or closed, mocking past speech or past thought. Publius Licinius Crassus had taken his own life in order to avoid his degradation by marauding bands that Marius had set upon the city for five days of carnage. He had won praise for refusing to see his enemy victorious and for using the same hand on himself that he had used on others. Crassus's father saved his family's dignity while he still breathed, but he failed to stop his death becoming a spectacle around the Rostra where he had so long tried to impose his will.

Crassus at this point was already in his late twenties, the time when a Roman political career might normally begin. But he had seen politics at close quarters since he was a boy and studied his city's strength and weaknesses in a serious household. He knew that Rome had owed its early success as a military state to its part-time armies of farmers who returned to their lands when each campaigning season was over. Faced with invading tribes from the far North Sea and an ambitious African king, Jugurtha, it had been running out of troops. The gentlemanly qualification for a volunteer force did not produce enough men. That, too, was a fact.

The threat from Jugurtha linked both the military and political problems. He was not a major enemy such as Hannibal of Carthage had been, but he was a master of guerrilla tactics in his desert home. He was equally a master of mass bribery at Rome to protect himself from invasion. Rome needed both highly trained professional soldiers and politicians prepared to use them. Until the reforms of Marius it had neither. Emboldened populist orators launched court cases against senators who sold their votes to keep Jugurtha safe on his throne. Convictions, however, were neither common nor effective. Jugurtha said that Rome was "a city for sale and would perish if only it could find a buyer." This minor African king was not alone in seeing a city whose past had been extraordinary but whose future was in doubt.

Gaius Marius, whose family had never held the consulship before, had led the campaigns at Rome against both the bribery of his colleagues and the old rules of army recruitment. After his success, the poor could join, be trained, and be paid. This was a clear advance. In future a new Jugurtha might readily become a new Hannibal, not just controlling the southern Mediterranean but threatening Rome itself. Romans never knew precisely why Gauls and Germans swept across the Alps, whether it was because of greed, hunger, curiosity, or having nowhere else to go. They might at any time come again.

Marius reorganized Rome's legions for greater endurance and mobility than before, each with a newly created eagle standard that gained the immediate force of myth, a totem to be defended to the death. They were to be a specialist infantry force: cavalry would in future be provided by local allies. These first new legions, led by Marius and his very different deputy, Sulla, defeated Jugurtha and the northern tribes. They also began a shift in political power that would reshape Crassus's life.

Crassus became notorious later for his remark that no man should be called rich unless he could finance an army from his own income. One of his first public acts would be to borrow, build up debts, and pay for one himself. But the paid legions of Rome did not immediately become private legions. Only the possibility of that problem was there at the start. Only gradually did Roman soldiers become more loyal to their paymasters than to Rome itself.

Crassus's father had liked to support the middle ground where he could find it, a preference he passed to his son. In some debates Publius had been more supportive of Marius, the outsider who was modernizing the Roman army, than of Sulla, the offender of the Parthians, who had come to lead the traditionalists of the Senate. From the Rostra he had backed new payments to attract new soldiers, a breaking of the link between land ownership and the legions. As a general he had lost a dangerous battle with some of Rome's dissatisfied Italian allies, learning in the worst possible way the weaknesses that needed to be fixed. He had promoted free food for the people and more rights for the Italians beyond Rome who, alongside the city poor, were increasingly strengthening its army.

Then gradually he had begun to see Marius's cure as worse than the disease, worse for both his family and for the city itself, in as much as he saw any difference between those interests. He saw Marius's own son, Gaius, acting as though he belonged to a dynasty of dictators, having an elected rival hurled from the Capitoline hill, sending the head of another as a gift and as a warning. Publius had attempted to raise troops for Marius's opponents in the nearby Alban Hills. He had criticized the chaos that change had brought, and the chaos had made his head, too, a prize.

Consequently, and suddenly, Crassus was in a new place in life. His father, Publius, had lost the first of his three sons before the main onslaught of Marius's terror began, and the second to the five-day fury that cost him his own life. Some said that Publius had killed his second son to save him from a worse fate. Crassus himself had by then already married the widow of his first dead brother. After his father's and second brother's death, Marcus Licinius Crassus became the first man of a family in bitter political dispute with those in power at Rome.

The name Crassus originally meant "solid" in Latin, although the family names of the Licinii also included Varus, which meant "crooked," and Calvus, "bald," which Crassus may have sometimes used as a disguise. Crassus's grandfather was called *agelastos*, a Greek name for a man who lacked a sense of humor. Each succeeding generation of the Crassi had at least one member who could boast a consulship, the annually changing office, elected by the people, always shared with another family, which in Roman eyes was the city's protection against anyone attempting dictatorship, monarchy of the eastern kind, or worse.

In Publius's consulship, when Crassus was eighteen, reform had been only tentative. He was best known for laws to regulate luxury dining and to ban magicians and human sacrifice. Eight years later, in his censorship, a senior role for vetting entrants to the Senate, he promoted laws against expensive perfume, a product both extensively used by men in the East and expensively bought from them, both aspects undesirable. He banned foreign wines, too.

Publius was a modest reformer in an age where moderation was in retreat. But he was successful enough in the traditional ways to win a triumph in 93 BCE, a procession through Rome in which his sons also had a part. There they could show the crowd the masks of his ancestors over more than three centuries, a claim that was as common among the politically ambitious as it was commonly unfounded, but no less potent for that. Certainty went back probably no farther than a consul during the defeat of Hannibal, but certainty was no requirement for show.

There was a vigorous range of the more recent Crassi. Lucius Licinius Crassus had been a master of the speaker's Rostra in Crassus's youth, a man rigidly intolerant of those who let down their family name, once pausing in a courtroom speech to abuse the passing funeral procession of a Marcus Brutus who had failed to match the best of his ancestors. Lucius was a traditionalist who backed reform and an orator whom even the high-minded Cicero praised as a model: Cicero would have liked more of the family to be like Lucius and had high hopes of the young Publius Crassus. Lucius's wife, Mucia, was famed, though not among the masculine masks of a triumph, for the antique purity of her Latin. One of the family branches had the added name Dives, meaning the rich, a source of confusion in later times since Crassus himself was not from the Dives side of the tree. While Julius Caesar would soon be hailed for his descent from the goddess Venus, no one ever saw a heavenly origin for Caesar's banker.

No family's history boasted its businessmen. In the halls of the great houses around the Forum many an ancestral mask was of a man who lent money, but no waxen face announced that fact. Rome's large and jostling senatorial class was banned from overseas trade by laws that, while often ignored, were not repealed. Banking was a trade that traversed many borders. It was best done quietly, as Crassus's mother had known. In 87 BCE he was newly prominent in an ancient family that, while not holding a united political view, was known for closeness, modesty, public service, and lack of extravagance; he was also a man on the wrong side of a revolution and with no option but to keep his own head down, to stay out of trouble and leave his father's head for the birds.

Behind Rome's northern wall were the last streets of the home that he knew he had to leave. There was the Via Salaria, the ancient Salt Road, and the Alta Semita, the High Path, the names reminders of when salt, not silk, was the precious commodity of trade and roads were footpaths when they were passable at all. There was the starvation chamber used for Vestal Virgins who failed their vows. Crassus had a cousin already designated to join that otherwise privileged band whose sacred flame held the life of Rome itself. Her name was Licinia, and soon, and for the future as far he could see it, he would have to remember her from afar.

To either side spread narrow alleys and tumbling tenements, homes of the city poor who were predominantly Gaius Marius's supporters. This was the part of the city that had been most crowded for longest. Crassus's great-uncle Lucius, who had died only four years before, knew what was needed to ease the burdens of those behind the Colline Gate: cheap corn, free corn when famine loomed, more cash in the economy, plots of land in the countryside, freedom from corrupt courts. Crassus's father had supported the same sorts of reforms, but Marius and his allies had offered more, or seemed to offer more. They had been better believed. Those who wanted to keep all their old wealth and power had become as determined as their opponents. The middle ground had been swept away like parts of the High Path by swamp.

Each side had its champion. Marius, whose family had never boasted a consulship, was a military modernizer who offered rewards for fighting Rome's enemies beyond the glory alone. Sulla was from one of the city's grandest families who had fought loyally alongside Marius in Africa until they had fallen out over the political spoils. Marius, the rugged old soldier, thought that Sulla, in his view a young, purple-faced libertine, was claiming undue credit for the capture of King Jugurtha. Marius was popular with the people, Sulla with senators anxious about how much farther Marius's reforms might go. Much greater than any ideology, or even interest, was the clash of ego and ambition.

A gulf between two men who wanted to be top in Rome had produced ready followers, a violent sequence of unprecedented events, a march on Rome by Sulla, a consul in 88 BCE, a march out of Rome by Sulla against Mithradates of Pontus, a western neighbor of Parthia who was expanding at all his neighbors' expense; and then, as soon as Sulla had gone, a violent return by Marius, maddened by the ingratitude of the citizens he had saved from grasping Italian allies, greedy Africans, and savage invaders from the North.

Crassus's father had supported both Marius and Sulla at different times. His death left no choice for his son who had been hardly more than an observer of politics until the lines of heads had become the attraction in the Forum that the people came to see. Crassus would fight for Sulla if he could. First, he had to stay alive.

He hid at Rome for some eighteen months. It was not so hard for an unknown young man to hide in a city at war with itself, around the poor citizens' Temple of Venus (the rich had their own on the Capitoline Hill), around the tomb where Vestal Virgins who broke their vows had once been buried alive, lowered by chair into the chamber with only enough food and drink for Romans to be sure that they were not the executioners. There was supposed to be no respect for the Vestals starved to death, no recognition of their spirits, but somehow there were always those remembering.

Nor would the horror brought by Marius be forgotten. Crassus wanted to be sure of that. Those who had put a spike through his father's neck would pay a price, maybe not the killers themselves (he did not know who they were), but those responsible. Rome was rotting. It was like a diseased body, with tunnels for veins and arteries, sweating pores and bleeding passages. The mouths of the dead rotted as though their words in life had been rotten, their behavior ever debauched. Rome was as it smelled. The odors and stains of Marius's city, no longer Crassus's, were the city itself, ever more so amid the continuing madness.

Among those fleeing Rome were Sulla's wife and children. Their destination was Athens, where they could deliver him the news. Crassus hid until the threat became too great. His own wife and children had to stay behind. All around them were the remains of rage, ashes that still flared to life and showed no signs yet of dying.

As Crassus crept away toward the walls, the air clearing as he passed the city barriers, his road ahead was in the opposite direction to the family of Sulla, north and west to Spain. With him were three friends and ten family slaves, enough for safety, not enough to look unusual or a threat. Spain was the country that he knew, which his father had governed, and where he might find safety until the state of Rome stood more in his favor.

CHAPTER FOUR

Inside the Cave

The principal biographer of the Roman world arranged his lives in pairs. The short life of Crassus by Plutarch, written around 100 CE, was paired with a life of the Athenian politician Nicias (470–413 BCE), a political fixer who lost a catastrophic war in the golden age of Greece. Both of Plutarch's subjects were fabulously rich from property and silver mines, both were more successful at home than abroad, and both could be used to illustrate the dangers of excess. This was the sort of comparison that Plutarch aimed to achieve.

Plutarch was a Greek priest and prose artist very proud of his right to a Roman name. Lucius Mestrius Plutarchus wrote his *Parallel Lives* to make political points about his own day: that Greeks could be just as good as Romans and, in the case of Nicias versus Crassus, morally much superior. Plutarch was a pioneer of the pointed anecdote: his Crassus was defined by greed; any generosity was always to serve his own ends; he was a man who might give a coat to his traveling philosopher, Polyhistor, but would always take it back when the trip was over. This moralizing portrait, drawn from good sources and bad, some writers who knew him and many more who did not, set the ground on which Crassus's reputation would rest for two thousand years.

In the Senate men might compare Crassus with his lifetime rival Gnaeus Pompeius, Pompey the Great, but Plutarch compared only Greeks with Romans, Alexander the Great with Julius Caesar, two good leaders of Sparta with Pompey and Sulla, whom Plutarch did not think so good. The saintly Roman king Numa, creator of Rome's calendar, its priesthoods, its Vestal Virgins, and other pillars of Rome's religion, was set beside the even more virtuous Lycurgus, mythical founder of Sparta. Marius was coupled to King Pyrrhus of Epirus, close across the Adriatic, who in the early third century came closest to conquering Rome for Greece, leaving posterity with the notion of the Pyrrhic victory. There was no other culture with which Rome could be parallel for Plutarch. Parthia was just one of many powers beyond the pale.

As Crassus was heading for his Spanish exile, there came news from Parthia of the death of King Mithridates II, probably little noticed at a time of Roman blood and gore at home. Mithridates' legacy to Parthia was an empire worth fighting for, expanded and secure, and a quarrelsome family keen to fight among themselves for it, a double inheritance that while not of huge interest to Romans would grant them almost a quarter of a century of freedom to ignore Parthia altogether. Internal strife and succession battles swiftly shrank the Parthian Empire, emboldened its neighbors from China to the Black Sea coasts, and ensured that Marius or Sulla or whoever took up their causes had no aggressor to fear beyond the Euphrates.

At around the same time in Parthia a man was born with whom Crassus came to be compared much more brutally than in any parallel critique, a general whom Plutarch called Surenas and whose pedigree, wealth, ambition, and private army were all comparable to the qualities of Crassus. So, too, as points of difference, were his youthful elegance and personal demands: a thousand camels for his baggage and two hundred carts for his mistresses. Surenas was probably not his real name, any more than his sexual demands needed so many suppliers, but it is the only name that has survived.

For more than a year Crassus stayed in Spain, a safe haven where a network of his father's loyalists kept him informed, as best as anyone could, about the struggle for the future of Rome that was taking place elsewhere. Sulla was with his army fighting King Mithradates of Pontus, the ruler attempting to gain the greatest advantage from the civil wars in Italy and Parthia. In 86 BCE Marius died, deluded that he was himself beside the Black Sea and about to defeat another enemy of Rome; the man of the people whose family had never held the consulship before had just become consul for an unprecedented seventh time.

Every Roman legion now had one of his bronze eagle standards, an innovation to motivate his new recruits. Mythmakers were already spreading the story that, as a country child, Marius had discovered seven eggs in an eagle's nest, one for each consulship, where an ordinary boy, or any other birdwatcher, might expect to find two at the most. The Marian faction was still in control of Rome, led by Lucius Cornelius Cinna, a subtler performer on the political stage than Marius had been, a man who preferred to conceal his ruthlessness rather than flaunt it.

These were years of frustration for Crassus. When Cinna took sole control of the city, he restored order as Marius never had. He was a distant relative of Sulla and might thus have bridged Rome's divides. He demanded peace within the walls of Rome, and financial security most of all, canceling three-quarters of debts and instituting new regulations over future loans. His ally, Marcus Marius Gratidianus, put into law a popular reform of Roman money, setting fixed exchange rates between bronze and silver, attracting criticism for appropriating rivals' ideas but much praise for the policies themselves. Silver and gold, hoarded during times of Italian war, returned to circulation.

Such outcomes, reliant though Crassus was on unreliable news, must have seemed wholly in his interests and in the interests of Rome. Yet he was no part of them. A young and ambitious aristocrat called Julius Caesar had married Cinna's daughter. He himself was an exile and still at risk. An assassin sent by Cinna, quietly and deniably, was no idle fear.

For eight months Crassus had to live with his companions in a secret cave. A local ally, Vibius Paccianus, would send over food for the cave dwellers to find and, according to Plutarch in his best, most pointed way, two "comely slave girls" who were told to enter quietly and say that they were "in search of a master." Plutarch always had difficulty with his Life of Crassus: too many of the scenes also had a part for Pompey and Caesar, and their Lives meant more to him. He did not like to repeat himself any more than necessary. Slave girls in a cave were new characters in a new setting, with the poignant addition that one of them was, as an old lady, still dining out on the exploits of her youth.

Then, suddenly there was news for the exiles that made a difference. Cinna was dead. Three years after Crassus had left his father's head in the Forum, he learned that Cinna, too, had found his assassin—among his mutinous army awaiting Sulla's return from the Black Sea. Marius was dead, and now, in 84 BCE, his more dangerous populist successor was dead. This made Crassus see an opportunity, even a necessity, to return to politics. If he had sat out the next phase of the civil war, he might never have regained his family's place.

Without orders, or even authority, from Rome, he began to raise a legion from his father's retired soldiers, tempting them with both the pleasure of revenge and the profit from being on the winner's side. That side had to be Sulla's, and Crassus needed to have as much force as possible to bring to bear, to make himself noticed and necessary.

The name of a Crassus still counted in Spain. Roman official authority in its largest province was weaker than at any time since its foundation. A small force soon looted enough to pay for a larger one. After threats against nearby Spanish towns and the sacking of Malaga, which refused his extortion, he had enough men and ships to leave for the province of Africa, no longer an exile but a general.

There he further reinforced his tiny army, refusing to cooperate with any mere legates loyal to Sulla (however grand they were), and sailed to Greece to put himself personally at the service of his new commander. Within weeks he had found his way to Sulla's side, helping to prepare an invasion of Italy to sweep away the popular government that had killed his brother and father.

Sulla was Crassus's opposite in almost every visible way. Each man had lost his father in his youth, but Sulla was twenty years older and as flamboyant and unpredictable as his new recruit was calm. While Crassus was dark and every Greek's idea of a young Roman commander, Sulla was pale and blue-eyed, his red-gold hair falling over a face that was lead-white and marked with blotches of purple. Beside the Black Sea he had looked more like a wild man from the North than like a Roman. To his new officers in Italy the would-be leader of the Roman aristocracy looked more like the comic actors with whom he had spent his childhood.

Sulla had been an economic reformer in his consulship, outlawing compound interest on debt and making it easier for small lenders to sue for what was owed them. Like Crassus's father, he had seen the need to rebalance the interests of rich and poor. But as a veteran of every recent war, he had gained the easy laxity of long service, cynicism, cruelty, and a common touch that Crassus never found in his whole career. The stain that ran from Sulla's forehead to his chin might have been with him from when he was born but was more likely a symptom of syphilis; it was a mark that seemed to have been earned in his life rather than given at birth. His soldiers loved him.

Sulla did not look or behave like a Crassus, but he welcomed a sign that a young son of the old aristocracy was on his side, a man of the next generation, more able maybe than their fathers. As Sulla gathered his forces around Brundisium for a second march on Rome, the young Marcus Licinius Crassus, even with so tiny an army, was welcomed by the man who called himself Felix, in Latin the favored one. Plutarch, even when comparing Sulla to the devious Spartan hero Lysander, ender of its great war with Athens in the fifth century BCE, took a less flattering view.

CHAPTER FIVE

Crassus at War

Three hundred miles from Brundisium, to the east of Rome on the other side of Italy's mountain spine, lay a vast pool of water that flowed in from the mountains but stood stagnant, with no outlet to the sea. The land around the Fucine Lake was sodden with its shifting overflows, flecked with foam and fish, its air misty with warm rain escaping back into the sky. Its inhabitants were the Marsi, men and women who for two hundred years had been formidable allies of Rome but in the recent Italian war had been even more formidable foes.

Sulla's war for Rome was a war for Italy, too. He needed not just to defeat Italians who had spent a generation under arms; he needed to recruit them. They had fought for rights as citizens and allies, made peace but had still unfulfilled demands. Even loyalists who had returned to the Roman fold had unfinished business. All saw Sulla's opponents as more likely to give them what they wanted. The southern allies of the Marsi, the Samnites, were already, it seemed, in the Marian camp.

Crassus's first job from his new commander was to change

minds beside the stinking waters of the Fucine. The Marsi had defeated and killed a consul in the Italian war. Their leaders spoke Latin; it was for the right to become part of the Roman world that they had so bitterly fought Rome. A few knew Greek, but many of their soldiers spoke only their own language. Latin was for treaties and promises; Greek was for stories; their native tongue was for the witchcraft of ordinary life in which their mastery was feared far and wide.

While Crassus might need only swords to hunt and kill among the Marsi, words would be needed to win them over. Their own words were a mixture of Latin that Crassus could understand and tongue-torturing curses that he could not. They worshipped Hercules as Herclo. They revered a snake-charming goddess called Angitia, a sister, some claimed, to Circe and Medea, the most implacable sorceresses of Greek myth. The Marsi were very like the Romans, but to a Roman it did not always seem so. The magic arts banned by Crassus's father in his consulship were potent by the side of the lake with no outflow to the sea. It was perilous to patronize the Marsi but inappropriate to treat them as equals. Money and the promise of money would have to talk. This would not be like recruitment in the province of Spain, where his father's name had done the work.

Crassus asked Sulla what sort of military escort he should take for this task, how many armed men to protect him against those around the Fucine who hated all Romans or who, if they had to choose between Roman allies, preferred the populist side. Sulla's reaction was not what Crassus wanted to hear. As though speaking very much to a junior, he barked that revenge should be Crassus's escort on the lake of mist and ghosts, revenge not against the Marsi but against the Marians in Rome: "I give you as an escort your father, your brother, your friends, and your kinsmen who were illegally and unjustly put to death and whose murderers I am pursuing." Sulla was not minded to hear excuses, still less excuses in advance. Crassus, he felt, already had what he needed to ensure his safety and return with what they needed for victory.

Vying for favor with Sulla were other young commanders. The man with the most troops and already the biggest reputation was Pompey, from Picenum on the Italian east coast, square-faced and confident, his hair curled high over his forehead in the Greek style. Like Crassus, he was the very young head of an influential family: his father had recently died, less dramatically than Publius Crassus, leaving him a sprawling network of clients in eastern and northern Italy. Pompey was not yet called "the Great," and never would be by Crassus except in the most extreme need, but Sulla was said sometimes to stand when the young man entered the room, ironically or not it was hard to tell. Pompey's aping of Alexander in appearance was an irritant and a challenge to his allies as well as his enemies.

Pompey had three legions from Picenum. Crassus had only his single Spanish legion, hardly at full strength when it arrived, newly reinforced by his hard-won recruits from the Marsi. Together they were part of a war of chase and seek, with many encounters, none of them decisive or even looking as though they might decide the outcome. The deaths of some five thousand Marian soldiers in Umbria decided nothing; the victors could barely bury their own dead before moving on.

Crassus and Pompey defeated the Marian general Gaius Carrinas near Perugia but could not prevent him from escaping toward Rome in a storm on the night after the battle. Crassus, without Pompey, took control of the nearby hill town of Tuder on the east bank of the Tiber but immediately had to face the accusation that he had looted its treasury for himself. The charge fell as another shadow of distrust with Sulla, the kind that would regularly fall against Crassus over his political life.

It was a war in which Rome itself seemed almost irrelevant. Sulla marched his men into a city that was almost empty, all politicians gone, and only the tenements of the poor still teeming. His clemency there won him useful friends. Sulla needed to encourage surrender from those who thought they would lose, as much as victories that came at too great a cost to himself. Then he quickly moved out from Rome and on. This was an Italian war. Crassus and Pompey swept through the northern territories of Cisalpine Gaul, which would be Italian within a generation. A united Italy, at a brutal price, would eventually be the prize.

Whether the start of the Roman Empire would come under the banner of reform or reaction depended on the sons of distinguished fathers, on Pompey and Crassus, who exceeded their inheritance, and on the young Gaius Marius, who did not. The elder Marius had not held back in the promotion of his son, having him educated alongside Cicero and married into the Crassi, to a daughter of Cicero's mentor, Lucius Licinius Crassus. He had sent him on assignment to Africa, where he escaped enslavement, it was claimed, like some mythical hero, by seducing the mistress of a king. He was a fierce defender of his father's achievements; some said that the consul killed beside the Fucine Lake in 89 was a victim, not of the Marsi, but of a squabble with Marius over whose family was the greater.

Despite being promoted beyond Marians of greater talent, including Gratidianus, the popular reformer of Rome's money, the young Marius never matched the young men on the other side. His name brought him the enthusiasm of his father's veteran troops but not ever the political control exercised by Cinna, the leader of

Crassus's enemies at Rome until his murder by his own troops. When the decisive battle came, the young Marius was thirty miles southeast of the front line, facing Pompey beneath Italy's greatest temple to Fortune at Praeneste.

Carrinas was the Marian commander at what came to be known as the Battle of the Colline Gate. But he, too, was barely in charge of an army swelled suddenly by some seventy thousand troops from the southern rivals of the Marsi, the Samnites, under their leader Telesinus, the least placable enemies of Rome, still at war from the previous decade, determined to destroy Rome or at least ensure a Marian victory and the gratitude of the winning side.

This Samnite leader, mythologized at Rome as a man of awesome terror, had allegedly declared that the only way to rid a forest of wolves was to destroy the forest. Hearing from spies that Sulla had left Rome almost undefended, he made a nighttime dash from Praeneste. An Italian war had come home to Rome – and to those inside the city, it seemed that Rome itself might even be destroyed if Telesinus, as alien to them as their enemies thousands of miles farther away, so decided.

Crassus, whose role in the war up to this point had been subordinate to Pompey's, played a decisive part in the drama at the Colline Gate. As the sun rose, only Sulla's supporters inside Rome saw the danger from the unexpected attack. They rode out to attack Telesinus and were routed. Those left behind braced themselves for their city's first fall to another Italian force, fearing that the reprisals of Marius might be as nothing beside those of this massive Samnite army.

Sulla and Crassus, marching to Rome themselves, could only struggle to get back on the offensive. Their cavalry arrived ahead of them, seven hundred lightly armed men who caused sufficient distraction to delay the Samnite assault. Not until midday did the main Sullan army arrive, briefly rest, and eat before forming their battle lines on either side of the Colline Gate. Sulla, irritable and impatient, took the left, Crassus the right in a long formation, neither man able to see the other. Telesinus declared the day to be Rome's last as the imperial power of Italy.

Sulla ordered his men to advance and quickly saw them smashed back. He rode up behind them, his white face visible above his white horse, attracting a shower of enemy spears as he moved leftward along his bulging line, which collapsed as he passed. Crassus knew nothing of the imminent catastrophe; his own line was holding firm. Those who saw the danger best were the veteran guards on the Colline Gate itself; when some of Sulla's soldiers tried to flee into the city, they dropped the portcullis that was their last defense, crushing onlookers and escapers alike beneath the same spears of iron.

Crassus's soldiers fought on into the night while faraway to their left Sulla was trapped in his camp, awaiting Telesinus's next move. Sulla had every reason to fear that the least disciplined of the Samnites, with their Roman Marian allies, would be already looting the Palatine. Then messengers arrived from Crassus. At an extraordinary time they made the most ordinary request: Could they stop now and take their food? They brought news, too, that Carrinas was dead and that Crassus was besieging six thousand escapers and awaiting instructions.

Sulla gave his assent to breakfast and replied that those who wished to surrender should receive safe passage as long as they slaughtered those who refused. The Samnites collapsed. Guerrilla warfare was their strength; they were devastating among the wolves in their own forest, less drilled than the Romans in lines of battle. Later that day outside the Colline Gate lay fifty thousand dead. The heads of Telesinus and Carrinas were on their way to Marius besieged at Praeneste. Young Marius saw the show from the city's walls and, while he still had the power to be obeyed, sent orders to his supporters in Rome that aristocrats on the side of Sulla be murdered. He then tried to tunnel his way to safety before killing himself, as Publius Crassus once had done, to avoid giving his enemies the pleasure of execution.

When Crassus entered Rome, he moved as a victor into the streets from which he had left as an exile. He passed the houses of men and women who had had high hopes of the Marians and now faced their worst fears. He passed the tomb of the vow-breaking Vestal Virgins, then the people's temple to Venus, and headed the short distance southward to the Venus of the rich upon the Capitoline Hill. He entered the Forum, where he had last stared into his father's eyes.

Sulla summoned what was left of the Senate to the Circus Flaminius, to the temple of the Italian war goddess, Bellona, built two hundred years before to mark the seeming end of war against the Samnites. Sulla did not intend there to ever be a Samnite war again; the survivors of Telesinus's ambitions, stripped of their treasure and their towns, would become loyal Romans or nothing, their language, like that of the Marsi, also slowly dying until only the most learned grammarians would see its traces.

In the temple of Italy's goddess of war, Crassus heard Sulla speak quietly, with no rise in his voice when the screams of their prisoners rang loud through the columns, some cries echoing from the marble, others dampened by plaster, a massacre in sound until six thousand were dead. "A few criminals were being admonished," said Sulla to his supporters, still not quite sure of the character of Marcus Crassus but extremely grateful.

CHAPTER SIX

Ways of Revenge

Now was the season of the settling of scores. While others took revenge with more head spikes and humiliations, Crassus had his own way to correct the past and control the future. He did not identify and pursue any of those who had hounded his father and brother to suicide. The elder Marius was long dead; so now was his son who had avoided returning to Rome in Pompey's chains. Cinna had done him a favor by being murdered; that was the death that had propelled his departure from Spain. There were no names to the Marian mob of five years before, some of its members slaves, who had torn apart the dead body of Publius Licinius Crassus and paraded its head on a spike in the Forum. There was no point in wasting energy on violent revenge.

Crassus took a more businesslike approach. On white boards throughout the city appeared eighty names of "the proscribed," those who had committed crimes in the cause of Gaius Marius or who might have done or whose heirs or other enemies hoped they had done. Proscription was a word originally used in Latin for seizing the property of debtors. These new proscribed did not have to be unlucky borrowers; for reasons that they might never know — political, personal, financial, or the most random misfortune — their citizenship, lives, and property became immediately forfeit to the victors.

Those who had enforced the Marian terror, those of them who decided to ride their luck by staying in Rome, were not wholly surprised. There was initially some relief at the small number. Eighty was hardly a massacre. Certainty was better than doubt until there appeared 220 more names. A man who laughed at the named one day found himself named the next and his head on the tip of a sword the day after that. There was a Venuleius, from the extended family of his mother. There was Marcus Gratidianus, well known to Crassus, the nephew of Marius and a popular campaigner who had become almost a cult figure for his plans to aid both rich and poor by a much-needed reform of the Roman currency.

During the Marian terror, Gratidianus had used a lawsuit to force the suicide of a prominent aristocrat whom Crassus also knew. This man's son was now focused on revenge in a way that Crassus was not, a way horrific even in the bloody aftermath of the Battle at the Colline Gate. Crassus may even have witnessed the execution himself, what was almost the human sacrifice of Gratidianus, a life lost piece by piece, at the tomb of the man he had driven to fall on his sword.

This son was not himself the executioner. The torturer's role, a debut in a career that would often overlap with that of Crassus, secretly and sinisterly for twenty years, was Lucius Sergius Catilina. Gratidianus was Catiline's own brother-in-law, as respected and wealthy as Catiline was not. Gratidianus wanted to improve people's trust in cash while Catiline wanted the eradication of debt, most of all his own debt. Catiline hated Gratidianus and, in the heated anarchy of Sulla's vengeful, victorious days, he acted upon his hatred because he could.

This vengeance, based not on politics but on pure opportunism, was many times retold by both those who were there and those who found it too terrible a story not to tell. Cicero could still describe the goriest details twenty years later, in a Senate speech that became central to the careers of both Crassus and himself. Gratidianus, ever the crowd pleaser, as his enemies could note, had been flogged through the streets, his arms and legs smashed, his ears cropped, his tongue wrenched from his mouth, his eyes gouged, until his head, still pleasing its audience, was presented before the ever-white face of the new master of Rome.

Sulla showed his pleasure in return. He also enjoyed the head of the young Marius, Pompey's gift. Sulla accepted the remains of his enemy's son with a joke from a Greek comedy. He had spent his youth with actors and could readily quote the line from Aristophanes' play *The Knights* about the dangers of a young man wanting to steer a ship before he had learned to row: "Before you seize the helm, first pull the oar, then stand afore and study weather lore."

Five hundred years before, Aristophanes had satirized the excesses of Athenian populism, the people's preference for being bribed instead of disciplined, their rejection of established leaders (like the wealthy Nicias, the leader to whom Plutarch would later compare Crassus) and love of rabble-rousers. The knights were the cavalrymen of Athens, older, wiser, and richer than the mob. Age was important. Men should learn from experience, respect their elders, and rise to the top in due time. That was the message.

From Sulla this might have seemed hypocritical. He was more dependent than anyone on the military judgment of the young, of Crassus and Pompey most of all. But if it was a hypocrisy, he was happy with it. Every actor was a *hypocrites* in Greek; there was nothing wrong with actors. Sulla looked for the last time into the eyes of the young Marius with a knowing nod to shared culture.

Not every reaction was as vicious. Others were more practical. The family of Gratidianus was linked to that of Crassus by arguments about law and business more than politics, rights to water for farming oysters, the best way to decide how many bronze coins were worth a coin of silver. It was by business, not by the brutality of violence, that Crassus took his opportunities in the terror that his part in Sulla's victory had made possible.

The financial opportunities from proscription lay in buying at public auction the property of the condemned. Large townhouses were cheap when so many of the senators who required them were dead or proscribed in exile, their wives barred from remarriage and their children from inheritance. Although the killer of a man named on the boards could claim a reward, the bulk of the assets became the property of the state, available to be sold for cash or credit to anyone who dared to buy.

This was not investment without risk. The auctions were public, the names of the buyers known as well as the source of the goods on sale. It was hard to predict how Sulla might feel about those who profited from the fifty thousand dead outside the Colline Gate. All business was a threat to a senator's reputation, and the buying of dead men's land might be a lasting slur. It could bring decades of hatred from the families who had been deprived of their hopes — and a more widely spread enmity from their friends. Nor could anyone be sure that fortune was not a wheel, with this year's proscribed becoming next year's proscribers, and this year's dictator, Sulla's new title, being next year's body in the Tiber.

This was the territory where Crassus was the master. He was

never the closest man to Sulla. Pompey had been rewarded with marriage to their commander's stepdaughter, Aemilia. This was a gift unattractive to both parties since Aemilia was happily married already and expecting a child: it did, however, suggest a dynastic future for Pompey, who had also been entrusted with a large army to mop up the last Marian resisters in Sicily. Crassus had no option but to endure Pompey's triumph, a reward that Sulla had allowed because, in Pompey's own words, "More people worship the rising than the setting sun."

Crassus was probably not disappointed when the elephants for Pompey's chariot, symbols of his great service in Africa, proved to be too big to pass through an arch along the sacred route, nor when Aemilia died in childbirth. Crassus's own family life was as secure as Pompey's was not. His primary focus was not yet on a triumph of his own. He was watching the auction rooms. He was beginning what would become a very different path to power.

The new terror was more systematic than the old. During the wild rage of Marius, Publius Crassus and his son had been unlucky. Sulla's revenge was different, a rigorous removal of popular radicals and those who had misguidedly given change their support. It required its own bureaucrats. And its bureaucrats required a regulator. Crassus seems to have become the head of a committee assessing individuals' loyalty to the new order, a place from which he might add or subtract names from the proscription lists.

This carried more risk than mere purchase at auction. It was never clear how carefully Sulla was watching while Crassus acquired great estates in Italy and silver mines to add to those of his father in Spain, each property with the slaves who made it profitable and, with better management, might make more profit still. Julius Caesar was on the proscription list—but, despite his populist appeal, his aunt being the young Marius's mother, and Sulla's well-justified reservations about his ambition, he somehow won a pardon. Crassus, rightly and wrongly, was increasingly seen as the financier behind the scenes for decisions such as this.

Sulla set up an office of his own household slaves whom he freed to fill Rome's need for administrators of government. Each one, following normal Roman practice, carried the names of the man who had freed them; Sulla's were thus called Lucius Cornelius and a proscribed man might wake up at night to see an armed band of arresting officers, each answering to the dictator's name. This was an eerie insecurity, as alarming for Crassus as for lesser men, as fitting for the stage as was so much in Sulla's life.

To be a dictator's loyalty commissioner was no guarantee that the dictator deemed a man loyal himself. Sulla had depended on Crassus but, as the terror continued, seemed hardly less suspicious of him than on his assignment to the Marsi of the Fucine Lake. A victory at the Colline Gate had not changed the instinctive view of a mercurial general who had become a no less mercurial dictator.

No one ever suggested that Sulla was jealous of Crassus, only that he did not fully trust him. There was a report from Bruttium, deep in the Italian south, that Crassus had added a man's name to the proscription lists because he wished to buy his property at a knock-down price, scaring away rival bidders by his reputation at Rome. This might not have been true. Bruttium was far away. Truth twisted with every mile. But it was the kind of behavior that was becoming attached to his name.

Pompey meanwhile strengthened his own place in Roman society by a new marriage to Mucia, an heiress of the Caecilii Metelli. His mixed reputation as a husband whose dead wife had been chosen for him by Sulla and as a promiscuous lover whose partners proudly boasted his bite marks on their necks was much enhanced by his joining a family from the oldest aristocracy.

Crassus had, by contrast, to endure a rare slur on his private life. He was accused of seducing a Vestal Virgin, Licinia, who was his own cousin, seeking to acquire her villa outside Rome, endangering her reputation, and putting her at risk of starvation to death in the underground tomb behind the Colline Gate. His accusers were well-known allies of Pompey. Crassus was acquitted but, as his critics pointed out, still managed to buy the villa. Licinia suffered no harm unless a continuing life as a Vestal were counted as such.

Crassus was not the only suspect in this sort of corruption case. One of Sulla's senior freedman officials, a Greek called Chrysogonus, was deeply incriminated in a plot to charge a son with murder to cover up the sequestration of his land. The case would launch the career of Cicero, a provincial lawyer then little known at Rome, who took care to point out that Sulla would be much too busy to engage in such triviality himself. Crassus, by contrast, said Cicero, would dance the full length of the Forum if he thought it would improve his chances of being mentioned in a will. This was the start of a long war of words between the two men, broken by occasional deals in politics and property, that would last until Crassus's departure for Parthia.

Sulla's own early wealth had come from the convenient wills, and even more convenient deaths, of a stepmother and a mistress thirty years before his dictatorship. Later, and decisively, he had grown rich from his dealings and conquests in the East, the most respected route to wealth at Rome. He had classical Greek sculptures and much of Aristotle's library. Sulla had no need to be envious of Crassus in any way, but he was interested in who was getting rich under his rule. Crassus was not as expendable as Chrysogonus or as popular or powerful as Pompey. His was a different kind of power.

Crassus was confident that while massive moneymaking might

damage his reputation, it would win him more friends in the end. He sold grand houses to those who wanted to flaunt their new wealth and status while despising their preference for display over discretion. He took on cases in the law courts, often very minor suits, for those who might be useful in future. He worked sometimes with Cicero, a powerful combination of two men, who both took the long view of power. He offered rhetorical training in his own house to those who might later be useful. He became a senator and a regular attender in the Senate, newly entitled to wear the same purple-fringed toga that his father and grandfather had worn before him, joining other replacements for those who had supported Marius too far down the path of reform.

Sulla's priorities were to restore the membership of the Senate and, more important, to restore its authority. In the balance of Senatus Populusque Romanus he wanted more S and less P. Under his new rules the Senate would control the law courts, the People could vote only on legislation that the Senate had approved, and those who wanted to become leaders of the People, their tribunes, would both have less power and forgo any further advancement in public life.

Crassus had no personal affection for Sulla. Politically, he was conservative but not a reactionary. He was as patient as Sulla was a man in a hurry. He was doubtful if the clock of politics could be turned back so far and so fast. Meanwhile, for Sulla the victor of the Colline Gate had become a mere visionary speculator. He began to distance himself from Crassus — and let that distance be known.

CHAPTER SEVEN

Parthian Faces

Firm news from Parthia was hardly less scarce in these years than it had been when Crassus was born. If ever Parthians were mentioned at Rome, they were still inhabitants of an idea more than a place. That idea was "the beyond": the Parthians stood beyond the kingdoms of the East just as the ocean stood beyond the borders of Spain. Definitions were necessary for all understanding (Aristotle had taught that), and it was hard to define Parthians in the way that Gauls, Italians, and Greeks could be defined. Gauls were strong, Italians soon to be just lesser Romans, Greeks cunning and cultured, the Romans, of course, pious and perfect.

It was far from clear who the Parthians were or even where they were. Their borders were as ill-defined as their national characteristics and depended, it seemed, on the determination of their monarch, a ruler who was absolute until, very frequently in the years after the Battle of the Colline Gate, he had not been. Parthians were fickle and probably servile, too, since both were general characteristics of the East. But real Parthians were rare at Rome;

so it was hard to be sure and, unless there was a threat to the interests of Rome, not even very interesting.

Orodes was the name of the latest king to claim the *bashlyk* of Parthia's nomadic founder, a combination of felt hat and scarf, as displayed by Arsaces I on his coins two centuries before. Arsaces had been an archer, and archery, a secondary art of war, was a national sport, it was said. Arsaces wore dangling sleeves, pleated trousers, and tight-laced boots; so too, to judge from their crudely cast coins, did his successor Arsacids, dynasts who fought sometimes with their neighbors, very successfully, but most often with each other, with success only for one of them.

They had adopted the common religion of the region, the division of the world between good gods and bad and the worship of Ahura Mazda above them all. His prophet was Zoroaster, who had lived four centuries before.

Sulla had been the first Roman general even to initiate a brief exchange of words. The encounter had not revealed much except that, when Parthians spoke, they mixed Greek with languages of their own. Their coins already suggested the same. Their theater included the same Greek tragedies, the same plots of terror and pity, that Aristotle had praised and explained. The Seleucid heirs of Alexander, whom the Romans had defeated and the Arsacids had swept away, had used the most grandiloquent Greek to express their fading authority: "the Great King, the legitimate king, the king of the world, king of Babylon, king of all countries."

The Parthians had taken over the bombast along with the Seleucids' claims to the mountain regions south and west of the Caspian Sea and the flatlands as far as the Euphrates. This bothered no one at Rome very much. The Romans were well used to discounting other peoples' grandiose claims to power. No Parthian had ever attacked a Roman.

Parthian money was maybe the most certain proof of who the Parthians were. Roman traders in silk and slaves knew the bronze Parthian drachmas with their ill-spelled Greek inscriptions, their changing heads, and the unchanging archer who sat on every reverse. Sometimes the archer's seat was a cone-shaped rock, "the navel of the world," a conceit they had adopted from the great Greek oracle at Delphi; sometimes it was a royal throne, a conceit of their own. The motifs ranged from those of a sophisticated Greek to a Scythian thug, from quotations from tragedy to quivers full of arrows. Money was more universal than language. That was a truth that Crassus did know. Money could turn anything into anything, but Parthians were still barbarians in borrowed clothes. The silver and gold of Parthia were legendary but little seen.

While Sulla was succeeding Marius, while Crassus and Pompey were rising to succeed them both, and Julius Caesar was still lower down the slopes of power, Orodes and Gotarzes were the names of those disputing for the Parthian throne. Each had his own slave army: all Parthian soldiers, apart from their armored cavalrymen, were slaves, perhaps the greatest proof of their inferiority to Romans. Other warlords had their own forces of makers and breakers of kings.

In around 76 BCE the name Sinatruces appeared in the traders' money trays, an eighty-year-old from an Arsacid family branch in their icy Scythian homeland. But by then neighboring Armenians had encroached deep into Parthian territory and Sinatruces' palace was a pile of ash. Not until 70 did Phraates III, father of the king whom Crassus would face in 53, begin the task of rebuilding an empire that for Romans had disappeared as far out of mind as it was out of sight.

CHAPTER EIGHT

Fire and Finance

Freed from Sulla's immediate entourage, Crassus could concentrate on getting and spending. The getting was from the misfortunes of Sulla's enemies, the spending on those who might take their place in the power structures of Rome. Cicero likened the getting to a harvest; the spending was like the distribution of free food to the poor. Crassus was an innovator at both.

A property did not have to be proscribed to come into his portfolio of assets; its value might be reduced for sale in various ways. A person did not have to be obviously powerful to attract his support; his eyes were on the wide web of would-be influencers in what would be a different Rome for the rest of his life, with wider access to wealth, broader opportunities for high office, and greater concentration of power. This was a seeming paradox that Crassus saw early as the truth to come.

When Crassus was a small boy, and Sulla was inheriting his first fortune from stepmother and mistress, a large section of Rome had burned to ash and dust. In a crowded city made of mud bricks and wood, with only a few stone temples to impress the future, an occasional cleansing by fire was as common as the diseases of the swamp that it dispelled. But in the great fire of 111 BCE, almost the entire city was burned, a bigger threat from within than any enemy without. The victims ranged from the temple of the Great Mother, Cybele, high on the Palatine Hill to thousands of rooms, shops, and bars. Flames flashed through the wharves by the Tiber, through warehouses of grain and oil, window to window through apartments sometimes six stories high.

A few years later an envious critic of Roman power, a historian and former slave called Timagenes, said that he always cried at a street fire because the Romans would build back better. But that lesson had not yet been learned. The scenes that Crassus saw as he toured Sulla's city were not so different from those in the years of his childhood. Fire precautions had sometimes been planned but rarely implemented. Rome had only the most limited fire service. Fire breaks wasted what was already expensive space in a city cramped within ancient walls. Fired bricks were available but costly. Mud was cheap. The first baking of a wall would often be the one that destroyed it.

The citizen voters had suffered the most, those who lived in the low-lying districts, selling what anyone would buy and selecting the leaders who they hoped would help them most. For those who lived on the hills there was sometimes more safety. A great fire was as political as a great marriage. It might presage nothing or immense change but, while the flames roared, it was not clear which. It was like a revolution — or a reaction to a revolution. Many lost their lives and fortunes, but the farsighted, the focused, and the bold might make catastrophe their friend.

In 111 BCE Crassus had been only four. Now, in his late thirties, death had propelled him to prominence among the Crassi; though duty had bound him to the leadership of Sulla and the chance to avenge his father's and his brother's killers, Crassus was less constrained than he had ever been in his adult life. The hero of the Colline Gate had no public office, no military command, no privileged role in Sulla's service. While Pompey was winning glory for himself at the edges of the empire, Crassus was free to make both fire and finance the source of the greatest fortune that Romans had ever known — and to use the money to compete for power as soon as Sulla was gone. Some thought that might be very soon.

Crassus took different lessons from his time as a leader of troops than others did. Roman elections were already run on military lines, with people voting in variously sized cohorts, each cohort having a single vote for a consul or other senior post: every male citizen had a vote, but not every vote was equal. Crassus saw how army methods might fill many gaps in civilian life, how the techniques of success in war could be adapted by a man of business. He made himself a master of managing slaves as though they were soldiers, training them, as methodically as though they were legionaries, to be builders, designers, and demolition contractors, organizing his forces in cohorts and centuries.

Soldiers understood technology. They knew how some metals could be hardened and sharpened and others could not, how blankets soaked with enough vinegar might save a city wall from the flames of besiegers, how water was siphoned from a river into a mobile tank, how high a pump could work, how a catapult could break buildings and remove ruins from a legion's advance. Crassus's slaves became soldiers of the streets. Crassus himself pioneered the business strategies of such an army, offering to buy cheaply from the neighbors of a burning tenement block, using his fire service as a form of insurance. The best tactic was always to stop short of pure intimidation: the seller ought to feel grateful that Crassus had allowed him to save something from otherwise certain ruin. He lost friends in the auction rooms and fire-wracked streets, but he also gained them—by ready loans at reasonable rates of interest as long as the repayment came at the agreed time.

If the debt could not be repaid, Crassus was ruthless. Freedom, life, and property might be forfeit. But his generosity was as rare among his peers as brutality toward debtors was common, particularly if they were poor or politically unimportant. His was a bargain that Romans understood. The problem for the city, and what was not yet called its economy or productivity, was that so few were prepared to offer it to them.

A loan from Crassus did not need to be taken or repaid in coin, which was always a scarce commodity; it could exist on a wax tablet, in the trust that came from being part of a network of trust. Crassus was not a banker in the modern sense. He did not lend for long terms. He did not put a price on the far future. He was not part of any system of public debt: no city, not even Rome, spent money that it did not have in the certainty that there would be new revenues in the decades to come. But he became a master of the nearer future. By concentrating more on finance than on the military, creating different ties of political loyalty, he opened new ways to exercise power.

In his personal behavior he was more ordinary. Crassus was modest in the way that his father would have approved. His sons were educated but not to excess or indulged in other ways. He gained the reputation for entertaining his clients, not extravagantly, but regularly. He had only one house for his family. He looked down on those who had to boost their status by palaces even if, maybe particularly if, they had purchased their palaces from him.

Here he stood in sharp contrast to Sulla, whose old life was as a libertine and who, as Crassus may have sensed, might shortly abandon dictatorship for full-time pleasure on his country estates, turning the clock back on himself just as he had turned back the clock of Rome. Crassus had been close enough to Sulla to know just how ill the dictator had become, the purple pustules on his face showing the rapid progress of a disease that could easily be explained by his rackety style of life even if its actual cause was hardly understood at all.

Sulla was finding it harder to defend his policies, both the injustice of the proscriptions and his changes to the government of Rome. Former supporters, not just Crassus, were becoming more cautious. Opponents were becoming more active. One of them was elected consul for 78 BCE, side by side with a conservative colleague in a common Roman way, railing against Sulla's "crime-stained cronies." Pompey was lending the critics support from afar. Financial and political fortunes would hang on the pace of opposition and Sulla's response to it.

Then suddenly, four years after the Battle of the Colline Gate, Sulla announced his voluntary retirement to his library and wine cellars on the Bay of Naples, inviting the whole city to a street banquet to celebrate, strolling the city streets as a private citizen, challenging anyone to prosecute him who dared. Pompey was still with his distant armies. Julius Caesar, then aged twenty-two, was not yet of any account, avoiding any risk from his aunt's marriage to Marius and raising ships for the Roman fleet by the Black Sea. He was also gaining the name "Queen of Bithynia" for allowing himself to be seduced by Bithynia's king. Crassus, despite being a "crime-stained crony" to some, was as surprised by the timing as everyone else.

Sulla's life of wine, women, and literature lasted barely a year before he reached the twenty-second volume of his memoirs and died. No one knew the cause. It was not a soldier's death or an assassination that a man with so many enemies might have feared.

Gossips picked their causes of death to match the depth of their disgust or admiration for Rome's white-skinned, golden-haired, purple-faced dictator. For every sympathizer who hoped he had enjoyed his last months of freedom with his new wife and his favorite transvestite actors, there were more who imagined the death that they thought he deserved, the rupture of his bowels and the decay of his inner organs so that lice crawled from his skin. Plutarch gave a full report.

Caesar said that Sulla, for all his literary efforts, had forgotten the basic ABC of politics in stepping down of his own free will. That, he thought, was not something a dictator should ever do. Crassus had studied Sulla both closely and at a distance. He had his own ABC of politics, and it would not be long before it was tested to its limit.

CHAPTER NINE

Problems with Foreigners

The Parthians were once Scythians, a people who lived farther north than the Syrians and thus were wilder, just as the Thracian Greeks were wilder than the Greeks of Athens, just as Britons and the Germans were wilder than those lucky enough to live in Italy. When some of the Scythians moved to become Parthians and the Thracians, too, moved south, they brought their wildness with them, just as the Syrians and Greeks brought their clever, softer ways to corrupt Rome and the West.

Crassus, like every Roman, knew that these descriptions were not universally true. There were few Scythians, Thracians, and Parthians at Rome, and although he knew enough Athenians and Syrians to know that fewer fitted their stereotype than did not, that changed very little; just as forever after, knowledge of individuals hardly at all hampered generalizations about a group.

Dividing one group from another was an ingrained way of thought. It was itself a way of organizing thought, a method used by followers of Aristotle, including the tutor who taught Crassus his philosophy and the clerks who assessed borrowers for Crassus's loans. How rich, how poor, how sick, how well? How influential, how good at baking bread? Some men were naturally good-tempered; others were violent, like the bulls on his farms whose owners tied hay on their horns to warn the unwary. Crassus was a realist: a man had to be cautious of ideas that were ideals. Eyes could deceive, but what one observed oneself should always have its proper importance.

The most important line of divide lay between the enslaved and the free. That was a discrimination that anyone could observe. It was everywhere and always had been. It did not have to be justified by philosophy. Even Romans who were close to their slaves — and there were many — did not deny its existence. Even the most uneasy accepted it. Slavery did not depend on race or place of birth, skills or the lack of them. At any single moment it was a simple fact backed by the law, by any nation's law, and by simple force for those, like the Mediterranean pirates, who lived beyond law. Just as anyone might become rich or lose a leg, anyone might be enslaved, freed, and sometimes enslaved again.

Thousands of Romans had been enslaved in the defeat of two of their armies in Gaul by northern tribesmen, the Cimbri, whom Marius had eventually driven away from Italy. Crassus was six years old at the time of the Battle of Arausio, when the sixty thousand Roman dead, according to the terrified view at home, were the lucky ones. One acknowledged truth about northerners (Thracians were deemed some of the worst) was their cruelty to their captives, their drinking of their blood, and their selling them back to fellow tribesmen even farther north to prison pits from which no enslaved Roman would return.

In Italy enslavement for debt was only recent history. The law still allowed various forms of bond-slavery for those behind in their repayments, private arrangements between lender and borrower that little troubled the courts. A chained ankle in a dark cell could be the temporary fate of the indebted if they lacked the right friends. Temporary might not mean short.

Even Julius Caesar, recently on his way back from his holiday role as the "Queen of Bithynia," had been captured by slave traders. He had suddenly faced in foreign markets a very different future from the one on which he was about to embark, saving himself only by persuading his captors that they would earn more from him in ransom than on the auction block. His brief enslavement ended with the arrival of enough silver to fit out a small fleet of pirate ships. The slavers' lives ended when Caesar returned with ships of his own and crucified them in revenge. As a gesture to his brief solidarity with the afflicted, he ordered the slavers' throats cut before they were displayed on their crosses.

Caesar had been persuasive or lucky. Other aristocrats might not be. The poorer rarely were. Freedom might hang by a thread for anyone — as everyone knew. The thread was cut most often for those defeated in massed battles. Scythians, Thracians, and Parthians took slaves when they won and faced slavery when they lost. That was the custom regardless of the truth of the lurid details. Roman conquests created millions of slaves, Pompey at this time the biggest provider, Caesar about to exceed him.

Crassus was the most imaginative in their use, an unusually creative user of slave labor, a skill that brought him the same mix of praise and suspicion as did his financial creativity. His workers, from the assessors of his loans to the architects of his houses, were drawn from the vast pool of Rome's enslaved. They were the most educated force in the city, probably the most likely to win their freedom. He hired them to others, teachers and scribes, copiers of Greek manuscripts and students of their learning: not even Cicero had his own scribes all of the time. But Plutarch, summing up a widespread view, praised Crassus's appreciation of working capital, human as well as material, without being able to make this much of a virtue.

It was a war against escaped slaves that tempted Crassus into his first military command since the victory at the Colline Gate. This was not an ideal return to arms, but he had little choice. No one else in Rome could both lead an army and pay for it, and the need was suddenly acute.

Pompey was not available for the task, even had his grandeur permitted him to take it. He was far away while a routine breakout from a training camp for gladiators was turning into a national humiliation; the Senate had put in Pompey's hands the responsibility for defeating two of the last Marians, one in northern Italy, the other in Spain. Crassus had not bid for either command. In Spain, where he might have had a claim, the opponent was Quintus Sertorius, experienced and dangerous, resourceful survivor in Crassus's youth of the devastating Roman defeat at Arausio, no less resourceful now; the Senate, nervous of yet again entrusting Pompey with a seemingly permanent command, saw no alternative, and Crassus had probably agreed.

While Crassus knew that he would have at some point to lead an army again, his immediate interest was still in acquiring wealth and influence with lesser risk. The constitutional rules that he and Pompey had so recently helped Sulla to enforce were proving unenforceable but could only slowly be safely stripped away. The Marians were not just showing their opposition under arms: there was rising dissatisfaction from Italians who had won the vote in Rome and wanted to use it, from the people's Assembly, which wanted its tribunes' rights restored, and from influential businessmen with a wide range of grievances who often looked to Crassus for help.

Crassus's problem was that to the traditionalists of the Senate, restored by Sulla, he was of the right class but too rich, too young, something of an upstart; to the business groups he was both sympathetic and superior, also a rival at the same time; to frustrated populists, some of whose aims he knew were right, he was one of those enemy bulls whose horns were tied with hay. In Latin the word for hay, *faenum*, and loan shark, *faenerator*, were linked back in the origins of language: the poor who owed Crassus money were doubly unlikely to attack him as they did the rest of his class. The priority of his time as praetor, the rung on the career ladder immediately below that of consul, had been the using of his influence, wealth, and lawyerly skills to improve his positions with all sides.

There were always local distractions that loomed larger in Rome than events outside. Lucius Sergius Catilina, the flamboyant bankrupt who had torn Gratidianus to death in the early days of Sulla's victory, had returned to prominence with another vivid intervention of the kind that too easily gripped the Senate. He was accused of sexual relations with a Vestal Virgin, a capital charge not only for the Vestal herself but for the perpetrator, too, an adulterous betrayal of the state. It took the full attention of friendly Senate grandees to secure Catiline's acquittal.

Crassus worked hard in the courts. He helped distant relations and close friends of Pompey and Caesar whom he wanted in his wider political family for when he might need them. He aimed to be closer to Cicero. Despite their differences they would spin the same web of dependency and gratitude over Rome.

Gradually the successes of a slave army both north and south of Rome began to focus the most distracted minds. The escape of

Spartacus and his tiny band, their attempt to cross the line between slavery and freedom, had led to an unanticipated war that had taken a wholly unanticipated turn. They had defeated Roman armies; they had support among some impoverished free farmers. No part of Crassus's personal strategy included paying for five veteran legions to fight the army of a Thracian gladiator, but failure to recognize that Spartacus even had an army had already done damage enough.

Crassus's new legions, recruited from men who had fought and won for Sulla, was a massive force, much more than should have been needed to defeat fieldworkers and cooks who, however focused and well trained their leader (and Crassus had a professional appreciation of those qualities), should have been crushed months before. But at the end of 73 BCE, Crassus's first year as an elected official at Rome, his landowning supporters — the very rich as well as veterans rewarded for military service — had come to see a problem for themselves as well as an inconvenience for others.

By the ineptitude of two consuls, Gnaeus Lentulus and Aurelius Cotta, both allies of Pompey, the escape from a gladiator school in Capua had become a rebellion of slaves from nearby farms and then a raging threat to thousands of farms (including many of Crassus's own) and now, in the agitated minds of the fearful, a threat to Rome itself. This was beyond any rational fear but no less real for that. A threat from the enslaved was an assault on minds as well as bodies, a reminder that slavery was both fixed and fluid. In a house or on a farm different sets of possessions were in collision, humans against other forms of property. It was a kind of madness, with a core of the harshest human reality.

Calm had to be restored before normal politics could continue according to Crassus's plans. The Senate was in support; the people agreed that an emergency demanded an emergency response.

While there would be no glory from merely winning against Thracian and Gallic slaves, there might be gratitude for saving the Forum from its first alien occupation in remembered times. Madness could be manipulated, maybe managed. Crassus saw benefit— but also little option—in stepping farther from the shadows he preferred, out to the open, to military command as well as paying the bills.

CHAPTER TEN

Spartacus

Crassus was notorious for sending his men to any part of Rome that was on fire. Some would buy cheaply the burning property; others offered cash for property nearby whose owners feared the spread of the blaze; others, his critics complained, would fan the flames or extinguish them in only what he owned. Speed and ruthless management were essential. The task of defeating Spartacus needed the same skills, rapid offers of pay to Sulla's veterans, the simultaneous finding of younger men to join the cause and threats to those who hung back.

His new armies grew like new city apartment blocks. Crassus paid for thousands of red woolen tunics, sleeveless padded vests, neck scarves, and sandals, the dull necessities that kept legions alive alongside the glamour of Spanish swords, decorated daggers, and spears. Before Marius made his reforms, a soldier brought to war his own shield and helmet; when an army was growing in a hurry, its recruits queued for common supplies from their commander.

The two defeated consuls slipped quietly back within the walls of Rome, a reminder of failure's price. Their futures would depend on the needs and whims of Pompey. Their defeated men were given a second chance under one of Crassus's junior officers. This, too, ended in rapid disaster in the wine- and chestnut-growing hills — in defeat from foes who did not fight in the ways that legionaries were taught to counter and in ignominious flight, also in the demand from Crassus that one in ten of the men fleeing from the slaves should be clubbed to death by their fellow soldiers, both the killed and the killers taking their own share of the shame.

For Crassus this had to be the end of the first phase, not the start of the second. "Effeminacy and laxity" had been punished by traditional means, wrote Plutarch without approval. Crassus needed the fastest possible battle, but Spartacus did not march on Rome, leading his troops instead south, ever better armed with weapons stripped from the dead, their aim, it seemed, to cross to Sicily for reinforcements from the vast slave population there, which had risen up twice before. There were alarming reports that his army now contained many free Italians, not just the poor but men who had been disappointed at Sulla's defeat of the Marians.

At the Colline Gate, Crassus had known exactly who he was fighting. It was the last time in his military life that he did. News of Spartacus's intentions was no more than a cloud of rumor, and attempts to apply reason where reason seemed absent from the start. Sometimes his adversaries seemed keen to flee Italy and return to whichever part of Greece, Gaul, or the Near East had been their home; at other times they seemed happier to loot and rape their way through territory that offered much richer rewards than anywhere in Thrace. Freedom and prosperity may have led in different directions. It was better for Crassus not to pretend to know which of the two they sought.

He expected his own troops to know precisely what he himself was thinking — and how they should learn what they needed to know. "What time tomorrow would we be striking camp?" a soldier asked him, with the easy sense of equality that good generals allowed. Crassus's reply repelled any such illusion: "Are you anxious that you won't hear the trumpet?" There was no more room for the careless in his army than on his construction sites.

His main weapon against Spartacus was itself a work of construction, a rampart and a ditch across the Scilla peninsula at the farthest toe of Italy, where the army of slaves and free was waiting to leave for Sicily in hired ships. His second weapon was less easy to see, the links of political finance with the pirate captains who alone had the ships and the power to take the rebel army across the straits. It was rumored that these pirate leaders, who controlled a virtual state of their own at sea, had made a deal with Spartacus; and then, for reasons unknown, the deal had gone. The pirates had had to decide between the profit of defying Crassus and appeasing him. Money was already "coined liberty," as a later writer put it, and the slaves did not have enough.

To motivate his disappointed men Spartacus lit fires against Crassus's lines, ordered charges through choking smoke. He crucified a Roman prisoner where Crassus's army could see every detail of the horror. This was also a warning to his own forces of the fate that could await them if they failed. Eventually a charge succeeded. The way of escape for Spartacus and his men was back through a single weak point in the long wall, a bold nighttime scramble but not a turning of the tide.

Crassus had to divide his force to match the scattered divisions of his adversary. He led himself the chase of Spartacus's Gallic lieutenants; they held the five eagles of the legions they had defeated since their escape from the gladiator school. The return of these standards would mean more in Rome than the deaths of slaves.

While Crassus was collecting his eagles, Spartacus scored one final victory before retreating north. Crassus ordered a rapid chase, and after a massed battle, this war that should never have become a war was over. Spartacus was declared dead, the story of his death as much a mystery as that of his life. There was no mystery about the fate of some six thousand survivors. There were questions about how they might be treated but only one answer that suited all of Crassus's needs.

He could easily have ordered them killed where they were captured. Their numbers were no greater than that of the Samnites and Marians whose screams had broken the peace of Sulla's first speech after the Battle of the Colline Gate. His troops would have obeyed the order, readily if they saw the slaves still as the enemy, less so if they saw the prisoners as the property of people like themselves. But it would be done and done quickly, and hardly anyone would ever know.

Or he could have chosen to offer them for their previous owners to reclaim. This would have been complex and slow. As soon as the issue was property and not a military threat, there might be calls for compensation and the kind of legal wrangling that was his normal work but not what he wanted as a victorious general. Even the most rigorous abuser of the enslaved might think long and hard before reintegrating Spartacus's fighters with those working their fields. If their previous owners were as careless as the overseer of the Capua gladiator school, some might even break out again.

Crassus owned silver mines in southern Spain, between the Baetis River and the sea. So did many of his clients and partners, directly or indirectly through shares or shares in shares. Exactly how many miles of low tunnels and mounds of red earth were in his financial empire may have been unclear: those that he had inherited from his father, those he had purchased from the proscribed, those that were collateral for loans. Mines and money were linked like nothing else, not just because coins came from the metals that came from the Spanish pits, but because mines were the solid center of webs of debt that grew ever more flimsy the farther they spread from such sure sources of profit. For Crassus the hammering through poisonous ores, the pumping of polluted water by screws and bucket chains, were probably no more familiar than were the mines of the mythical Tin Islands for his father. What Crassus did know was that the deadly soil and sulfur-soaked air created an inexhaustible demand for the kind of slaves whose strength had once made an army.

A few weeks in the mines would end the last lives of Spartacus's fighters and recoup for Crassus some small part, at least, of the vast fortune he had spent on their defeat. But most Romans would never know that his industrial executions had ever happened; those who did know would be the owners of rival mines, ever keen to complain that Marcus Licinius Crassus was yet again enriching himself from assets that belonged to Rome.

Crassus wanted neither mystery nor dispute about the fate of his prisoners. Death by crucifixion was illegal for the free; it stood on the line that made a man a slave. A man dying on a wooden cross had no wounds as a soldier would have wounds; his feet were in the air, a final offense to the Gods; his death was slow enough for thousands of other slaves to see it and take heed.

Crassus made his choice — and implemented his decision with the care that he demanded when designing a house, a plan of battle, or a web of debts. The survivors of Spartacus's army were marched from Capua to Rome along the Appian Way, with a pause every thirty yards for the last man to be hauled up on to his cross. Those at the front never knew what was happening behind them.

They did not riot or require costly security. There was no time or mood for Caesar's kindly cutting of throats before the days of desperate pain began.

This mass crucifixion beside the busiest road in Italy was an unprecedented act, requiring power of organization as well as brutal cruelty, perfectly characterizing Crassus in the eyes of his supporters and critics alike. As a follower of Aristotle he knew the virtue of moderation. But moderation was a principle applied differently for those born enslaved or taken into slavery — even when it was applied at all.

The sensitive in Rome preferred to look the other way, putting the line of crosses from their thoughts as they put aside any fear they might once have had about the war itself. They had other routes to the south. Once any danger was past they wanted an event that had never happened. Once the birds had eaten the bodies and the wood had fed the fires of the poor, there was evidence of no event at all.

Crassus returned to Rome. He was right that the defeat of a slave army would bring him no triumph. Spartacus's force had been as alien as any defeated by Pompey, as any bands of Spaniards, Gauls, or barbarians from the Black Sea. But it had also been domestic, unworthy of the highest military honor, in some minds worthy of no honor at all.

Pompey himself was on his way back to Italy from Spain and would certainly be awarded the triumphal parade through the city streets, a commander's chariot ahead of his captured prisoners and treasure. His main opponent had been a fellow Roman, but Sertorius's Spanish allies were sufficient cause for Pompey's to be judged a foreign war.

At the end of Pompey's journey home he had found and killed

a few survivors from the slave army's defeat, allowing him to claim that it was he who had ended the miserable affair, both minimizing his rival's achievement and claiming part of it. Cicero, soon to be a dangerous enemy of Crassus, backed Pompey's claim. The victor over Spartacus had to negotiate for a minor show of his success, an ovation, in which he was allowed to lead some of his soldiers through Rome on foot.

His friends in the Senate decreed that at his *ovatio* he could wear the laurel wreath of the triumphant general rather than the usual myrtle wreath. Laurel purified a man against revenge by the spirits of those he had killed. Myrtle was a mere scented leaf of Venus. To Crassus the difference was worth making clear.

The result was still a poor reward. He had the right garland for his head but not the great parade that led to the political summit. Pompey still stood far above him in the public eye. He could console himself only that he had returned to his soldier's past, he had returned in safety, and he still had his men under arms, a potent lever in the political battles to which he had returned. Money, not myrtle or laurel, was "the sinew of war," and Crassus now had men and money under his control. His status was much closer to that of Pompey than it had been before. With Spartacus and Sertorius dead, Rome had two preeminent men, each with a preference to dance around the other, not to fight, and a set of Sulla's constitutional rules for which both had once fought but which now they would together dismantle.

In a bizarre election campaign to become consuls for the following year the canvassing was by vacuity and violence. Two armies stood by to encourage support for their commanders. Pompey was an accomplished rule-breaker. He was not a senator and, at the time when the normal garnering of support among senators and people would take place, was not even in the city. Crassus's men could not match those of Pompey, but the double intimidation was enough to discourage rivals.

When Crassus and Pompey stood side by side they chose each other, reluctantly but with a sense of necessity. They were the only choosers. The Senate and the people merely stamped a label of respectability on what was put before them. A pattern of the Roman future was taking shape.

Pompey did not much want his old rival beside him. He wanted a bland obstructer from the ranks of the Senate's traditionalists even less. Crassus was anxious that Pompey might still favor a less powerful, more pliable partner than himself. He, too, saw no option but to accept what he did not want. His long and expensive efforts to buy support among the voters could not be allowed to count for nothing. If success could come only in the retinue of his rival, so it had to be.

If the election had happened under the usual rules, Crassus and Pompey could both have boasted their descent from great consuls of the past, their defense of Romans in trouble, their demonstrable victories in war, the traditional arguments placed before the electoral colleges. But in the autumn of 71 BCE, a vigorous presence of victorious troops beside the city walls was an argument that mattered more than any of those. No other candidates stayed the course.

Once elected, Crassus countered Pompey's greater popularity as a general by promising free food, a public feast of ten thousand tables in the streets of Rome, and a tenth of his wealth to the Temple of Hercules, the half-man, half-god who had long held an appeal to the powerful at Rome. The party was the most extravagant since the retirement of Sulla. The gift to Hercules was, in effect, a tax payment to public funds. Then Pompey planned games in honor of Hercules, a competition to impress in which the people of Rome were clear winners.

From their observations of politics since Sulla's departure, both Crassus and Pompey had come separately to a shared agenda. The P in the Senatus Populusque Romanus had been too far trodden down, and the S had been too far puffed up. Under their joint reforms, agreed between them amid much personal suspicion, the P regained the powers for its elected tribunes that Sulla had taken away, and the S lost its exclusive control of the courts. But the final letter did not represent what it had before. To be Romanus meant increasingly to be ruled by the men — and then the one man — with the most loyal army.

Pompey looked after his allies who had so spectacularly failed as consuls in the first phase against Spartacus. Proof that loyalty to Pompey was more important than incompetence in battle, Cotta and Lentulus advanced to the censorship, an office that Sulla had abolished, from where they weeded out sixty-four senators whom they deemed inadequate for their responsibilities. Italian voters, whom Sulla had feared would favor radicals, were enrolled onto the electoral lists.

Pompey won most of the credit both for restoring the power of the people's tribunes and for extending the franchise throughout Italy. Populism was once more on the rise. Holding to the people's agenda was no longer the danger it had been. Julius Caesar, a young military officer on his way up the political ladder, felt free for the first time to celebrate his family connection to Marius, putting down a marker for his future place in Rome's debates.

Crassus saw the possibilities here as well as the dangers. He thought that he could turn trouble to advantage. While Caesar sought military glory in Spain, Crassus began to see him as a power he could use to balance that of Pompey – by loans from himself with which Caesar could buy votes and advance them both further.

As Pompey became more and more the people's favorite, the open political space for Crassus was with the Senate. He began to consider marriages for his own sons with the Metelli, a many-branched aristocratic family with daughters who might help his future: Mucia had already burnished Pompey's credentials while bearing him two sons.

Crassus had no choice, however, but to disband his army, for which he had no more military use. Those legionaries who did not want retirement would soon have the chance to go east with Pompey. Only his massive wealth, war's essential sinew, was secure under the new settlement of Pompey and Crassus. There would be no compensation for the family fortunes looted under Sulla's proscriptions. His lands, houses, and mines, once owned by supporters of Marius, would remain as reserves for his empire of banking and trade.

Moneylenders were forced to reduce burdensome interest rates to eastern cities and forgive some debts. Pompey had a diplomatic agenda that he did not want disrupted by Roman policies that had forced the sale of sons and daughters into slavery, the sale of sacred art, and sometimes the freedom of the debtors themselves. But this was all at a manageable cost to Crassus.

Pompey's ascendancy was temporarily impossible to challenge. Crassus was hardly more than his political fixer. When he had soothed the Senate, large numbers of whose members were already in his personal debt, he had to soothe the anger of the moneylenders. His only option was to return to playing for time. His plan was again to gain mastery of Rome by being in Rome.

Pompey, as Plutarch later wrote, saw that "life in the robes of peace had a dangerous tendency to diminish the reputation of those whom war had made great"; he would stay in Rome only as long as he had to, lobbying for the military commands that he needed. Crassus took the opposite view. He hoped that he could hold onto his new military reputation alongside his life in the robes of businessman and banker that suited him best.

On their last joint meeting with the people's Assembly before giving up their consulships, a man jumped up on to the speaker's Rostra and shouted that Jupiter had sent him a message in a dream. He was not to allow Pompey and Crassus to stand down from office until they had proved they were friends. There was loud applause at this, and Crassus was the first to react, moving quickly to shake Pompey's hand. Pompey seemed more shocked than pleased, perhaps suspecting that this was a plot to make him appear ungenerous, mollified only a little maybe by Crassus's speech that he was proud to be a friend of one who so long ago had won the title of "the Great."

CHAPTER ELEVEN

Eastern Questions

Pompey was to learn much more about Parthia than Crassus ever did. In 67 BCE he took responsibility for clearing the seas of pirates across the whole of the eastern Mediterranean. There was great reluctance to let one man have such widespread power, but Rome's traders were losing too many ships; the food supply for rich and poor was strangled; tons of oil, wheat, and slaves were being intercepted every day and taken to cliff-top fortresses. Pompey deployed subtle force and brutal diplomacy, listening to stories from the East, impressing all sides by his negotiations and calibrated violence. Even his legates, Lentulus and Cotta, spectacular failures in the first phase against Spartacus, played their part in an extraordinary success.

Crassus had to watch his rival become a popular hero, the conqueror of what was, in effect, a nation afloat, a feat that won him not only admiration but information. His next task from his grateful fellow citizens was to remove Rome's excess of soldiers, to finish a stuttering war against King Mithradates of Pontus, and to stabilize the neighboring kingdoms that stood, ever uneasily on the edge of peace and war, between Parthia and the provinces of Rome.

Pompey traveled east and held his own talks with the Parthians. He cajoled King Phraates, hobbled by civil war himself, to invade Mithradates' ally, Armenia. Phraates gave his daughter as wife to Tigranes, the would-be Armenian king, but failed to gain the territory that he hoped for. He succeeded only in providing the distraction that Pompey desired. Pompey offered the Parthian king some small recompense for his efforts and then refused to pay even that. This was the kind of rough diplomacy at which Pompey was beginning to see himself a master. In 66 BCE there was a first treaty between Rome and Parthia. Crassus, corralled on the sidelines, could only be patient.

Pompey's plan was to create three zones beyond the eastern shore of the Mediterranean, the first the wholly Roman provinces of Pontus, Syria, and Cilicia; behind these would be a line of rival independent kings, in Galatia, Cappadocia, Armenia, and Commagene, countries large and small, all looking suspiciously at one another and fearfully at Rome. Parthia would be kept behind this line, free to expand east when it could but constrained on its western side behind, as Pompey put it, "Whatever border I determine to be the just one."

A meeting between Roman and Parthian troops gave their commanders a first sight of each other's strengths, a wall of legionary shields and a whirling buzz of bowmen on tiny horses. The Parthians had giant horses, too, armored from hoof to head, ridden by armored men carrying each a single long spear. These had a Greek name for things that were completely enclosed, *cataphracts*, clumsy as they seemed to Roman eyes; the two sides came close and retreated. The immediate argument was over the fate

of Tigranes, the potential king of neighboring Armenia, father of Phraates' granddaughter, now a Roman hostage.

This meeting led to no improvement in the fate of Phraates' diplomatically married family, only to the possibility of fighting between Parthia and Rome, a tiny glimpse of what was to come. Pompey's men, under one of his officers, crossed back into Roman Syria, stopping briefly on the way at Carrhae, a small, mud-walled town on the flat plain between the upper reaches of the Tigris and Euphrates, a place then of no particular importance to a Roman.

While no one had made more money than Crassus from the civil wars of Marius and Sulla, the fortunes of many other old families had fallen to less than nothing. In the big houses above the Forum, including those built and owned by Crassus himself, were angry men who would welcome another throw of the political dice; some were agitating for it. Crassus was watching with particular care the bankrupt aristocrat Lucius Sergius Catilina, whose most public act of violence had so far been the torture and dismemberment of Gratidianus, the currency reformer, in the weeks following the Battle of the Colline Gate. Like Crassus, Catiline operated more in secret than in plain sight. His dishonors included the killing of his own wife and the bribing of judges with money that he didn't have. When Julius Caesar was the acquitting judge, any help from Crassus to Catiline might achieve two objects in a single transaction, making both indebted men more dependent on their banker.

Catiline had ambitions for an even bigger cancellation of debt at Rome than had been granted to the desperate cities of the East. He had hoped to stand for the consulship in 66 BCE but had been blocked by corruption charges and had spoken, rather too freely, of a massacre and coup to get his way. Crassus preferred, when he could, to know his opponents rather than destroy them. He chose to keep Catiline close. He could imagine times when he might need him.

He needed a mob in 65 BCE to disrupt a major extortion trial. The accused, Gaius Manilius, was an ally of Pompey, but Pompey was not in Rome to protect his ally. Crassus was happy to use his thugs on the street to fill the gap. Even when the trial went ahead and Manilius had to flee into exile, Crassus got the credit for his efforts. In the meantime, Pompey was still away. He was important, but he was not everything. He had become impossible to control and might surpass Crassus in wealth as well as warfare if he achieved his eastern ambitions. But on distant campaigns anything might go wrong.

Crassus saw a much less risky foreign adventure for himself. He raised an old argument in Rome that Egypt should become a province, perhaps under the governorship of himself, rather than a friendly independent kingdom. The wealth of Egypt would more than match anything that Pompey could win in Armenia and Pontus. Nor, if Crassus were in charge, would the fertile fields by the Nile be available as rewards for Pompey's troops; Pompey would be as irritated as Crassus would be enriched.

It can hardly have come as a surprise to Crassus that the Senate saw this prospect all too clearly and, as in the past, preferred that none of its members should be in line for such a prize. Cicero, admirer of the young Crassus but hostile to the old, used his oratory to lead the opposition with vigor. A weak foreign king who would pay tribute direct to the Roman treasury was a safer option than a strong governor who might unbalance politics at home. Ptolemy the Fluteplayer, father of the then unknown Cleopatra, was a perfect pharaoh. Undaunted, Crassus focused on what he could try to control, the next generation of dice throwers who might destroy everything. Julius Caesar's election as Rome's chief priest, in charge of the political as well as the religious calendar, would be a costly undertaking even for Crassus.

Catiline was popular—and not just because he bought votes, with promotional beakers of wine for those who sometimes had to spend hours in line to express their preference. The promise of a fresh start, free of debt, for everyone's personal finances had broad appeal among the people who already preferred Pompey to Crassus. If Catiline were to succeed in becoming consul, Crassus would be in a key place of influence. If he were to fail, Crassus did not want the blame. As long as Catiline could be guaranteed not to achieve his policies of eradicating debt, it was better to seem to be on his side than to campaign against him. Crassus was confident he could guarantee failure for so radical a measure, but he did not want the credit for doing so.

Despite the popularity of himself and his plan in the tenements behind the Colline Gate, Catiline was not elected. The electoral college gave the same weight to cohorts in smaller, richer areas as in the larger, poorer parts of Rome. If there had been a more direct democracy in Rome, as there never was and never would be, Crassus would have had less influence and Catiline might have done better. Instead, Catiline saw a rural rebellion that he could turn to his advantage, gave the farmers one of Marius's old eagle standards, and launched a revolt against the state.

Unlike Caesar's rebel forces fifteen years later, Catiline's were chaotic and small. He threatened a massacre of leading Roman citizens, including Crassus, although some thought that Crassus had invented the threats to protect himself. Betrayed at every point, Catiline died in battle at the head of his rebels, bravely it was said, in the best tradition of his ancient forebears. That bravery might have been better recognized had not Cicero, one of those successfully elected for 63 BCE, decided on a series of speeches to present himself as the savior of the city against unmitigated evil; an orator and philosopher rarely had the opportunity to appear as a Pompey or Crassus, and Cicero took his opportunity at great and much quoted length.

Crassus offered his house as a temporary prison for one of the surviving plotters. Caesar and four others did the same. This would be a useful public service if anyone suggested that the jailers were themselves part of the plot, though dangerous if the prisoners somehow escaped. This house arrest was not a lengthy responsibility. Cicero ordered executions without trial, a decision that brought him glamour and some small sense of what it meant to be a military commander. It took five years before Cicero had to pay the price for this fame and self-esteem, a prosecution and exile at the hands of those who thought Catiline a people's hero.

For most of that time, Crassus stayed in the background, where he most liked to be. He had a *secundarium,* a stand-in, Quintus Arrius, who represented him on the lesser political stages. A man called Lucius Tarquinius who dared suggest that Crassus had been sending support to Catiline ended in prison chains. Crassus's most prominent public act was to approve the marriage of his son, Marcus, to Caecilia Metella of the Metelli family, strengthening his links with the most conservative leaders of the Senate at the same time as Pompey, an enemy of Metella's father, mildly irritated at not being asked home to crush Catiline himself, was ever more the people's absent favorite.

CHAPTER TWELVE

The Nature of Money

Aristotle had used the word *economics* for what in future centuries became known as *politics*. Politics was what Crassus's tutor taught. Money was, by contrast, a household matter and sometimes, as rarely as possible for Crassus and Tertulla, the household had to be moved. Gold and silver had to be bound in chests, piled on carts, pulled by oxen, protected by slaves, and loaded onto ships, not all on one ship, an enterprise hard to justify and even harder to hide.

A year after the death of Catiline, Crassus feared that his years of control through cash and credit were coming to an end. Pompey was planning to return to Rome, and there seemed every possibility that he might copy the example of Sulla. Crassus had no great regard for Pompey's originality as a politician, however inventive he always seemed to be on the battlefield. Dictatorship and proscription might be his easiest options. Crassus did not want to be the most tempting target.

He decided to leave Italy. He might have gone to Spain or to southern Gaul, both places where he had supporters. Instead, he chose Asia. For one gift from Pompey, he could be grateful: pirate captains no longer controlled the seas. Roman ships could sail the Adriatic with hindrance only from heavy weather.

He did not have much time. Pompey, as was well known, was already preparing his own vast transfer of wealth from east to west, golden thrones of conquered kings, mountains of the coins that bore their heads, piles of looted pearls and precious stones, statues of long-dead Greek heroes, long lines of living slaves from the places whose kings he had created and whose borders he had drawn. Romans would see all this when the man whom he had first met as a fellow young officer with Sulla celebrated his second triumph. The "new Alexander" was rumored to have captured the original red cloak of the old and would likely wear it, tossing coins to the crowd, turning money into power, turning the streets into streams of blood if that was what the "new Sulla" wanted to do.

Money could become anything but not always quickly. Crassus could mortgage his mines and lands for cash and promises of future cash but not at the best price if it was known he was leaving Rome and might never return. Most of Crassus's wealth was in wax tablets, in handshakes, in subtle threats, sometimes not-so-subtle threats. Aristotle had called the lending of money unnatural and wrong (money was dead and should not bear fruit as does an apple tree), but Crassus's tutor could ignore what his master might not want to hear. The debt tablets were most of what Crassus owned. They could come to Asia, but a handshake was worth less, maybe very much less, when the hand that gave it no longer held power.

Coins could be carried. The smaller might be needed on the journey. Aristotle was right about that part of his subject; coins were wholly a household matter even when, despite the efforts of the wretched Gratidianus, torn to pieces by Catiline, they were not what they seemed to be. Not until a sestertius or a drachma was melted was its mixture of metals known. By then it had ceased to be usable for buying bread.

For buying politicians coins were no use, except perhaps when someone like Catiline wanted to stand drinks for voters waiting in line, his name on every cup. A consulship cost more coins than could be kept in a hundred money chests. Rome had no paid politicians, nor ever had there been the slightest suggestion of them. The post of Pontifex Maximus, Rome's senior religious leader, came with a house in the Forum, the only house, but that was a rare perquisite. Those who wanted high office had to spend to win votes, both legally and illegally, and hope to recoup their outlay by looting a province the following year. Opportunities for political newcomers, like Marius or Cicero from outside the old families of Rome, simply made the contests more expensive. The more open the competition, the higher the costs.

There were far more opportunities for an ambitious politician to spend money than to acquire it. Investment, election, and a province equaled success. Investment and failed election might mean disaster; successful election followed by the wrong province might be worse. A bankrupt could be banned from any future office. The business of politics depended on single calls, right or wrong, hardly different from a battlefield.

While Catiline was bankrupting himself for advancement, Caesar had risked the same fate, spending colossal sums of Crassus's money, and that of others, to be elected to Rome's high priesthood, a role that came not only with a well-placed house but with the right to veto dates for meetings and elections. His reminder to voters that the founder of his family had been Pontifex Maximus in legendary times had been nothing like enough. The stakes were much higher than the status of the first Iulus in the years between the Trojan War and the feats of Romulus. A rival had offered to pay off Caesar's massive debts from past campaigns if he would withdraw from the contest. But Caesar had not withdrawn.

Caesar stood for the office of high priest and won. He now had the only house in the Forum and the right to speak for the gods in useful matters such as the dates for elections. Crassus had won a greater hold on a powerful friend and a repayment promise that would be redeemed at some point even if in Asia it might not be worth what it was in Rome. Money could become anything and nothing.

Crassus did not stay in Asia for long. He was soon embarrassed that he had ever gone. Cicero, forever of the view that the only good Crassus came from the next generation, took full advantage. There was not much that Crassus could do to change the story of his departure laden with cash: perhaps he had had urgent business abroad, a deal that could only be conducted face to face; perhaps he had wanted to shame Pompey for driving him into exile; perhaps he had never been afraid of Pompey and had left Italy in order to negotiate with his rival, not escape him. Later, when Crassus, Caesar, and Pompey were dividing the Roman world, some might come to believe that last claim, but at the time it was all too clearly untrue.

Crassus was still afraid when, in December 62 BCE, well past the end of the season for safest sailing, Pompey brought his fleet into Brundisium. This was the only harbor on the east side of Italy that could cope with such a vast show of force and its rewards; it was also the only place through which a hostile invasion could come. Crassus was not alone in fearing that the people's hero, weighted with the wealth of the East, might prefer dictatorship to the dreariness of everyday negotiation with the Populus and Senatus of Rome. He was not alone in being wrong.

Pompey's soldiers disembarked and, each with his share of the spoils, disappeared quickly into the countryside of Apulia. Their leader traveled to Rome along the Via Appia with only a few friends for company, almost as a private citizen, "as though returning from a foreign holiday," as Plutarch put it. He attracted such crowds of admirers along the way that "if he had had any revolutionary ambitions he would have hardly needed his demobbed army."

In Rome Crassus's fellow senators, and the people's Assembly, heard a speech that was as modest in tone as it was in content, even a disappointment for those who still saw benefit in a new act of political drama. If Pompey had the Senate in his thrall as well as the people, the S as well as the P, there would be no room for Crassus or Caesar. Crassus's prospects were the worse of the two. Caesar was younger and could wait for his consulship; Pompey might help him get it. Crassus was already at the top of the ladder of honors and needed a Senate hostile to Pompey if he was to be Rome's "first man," its principal citizen by common agreement and consent.

The Roman Republic had been built on the principle that no one should ever be first; there were always two consuls, two chief executives with equal authority, often voted in to be curbs on each other's enthusiasm. To be Rome's "first man" was to hold an unofficial title. It meant certain privileges in Senate debates but, more important, the certainty of being acknowledged as first. Pompey did not want to give Crassus that opportunity.

Pompey wanted the role for himself. He wanted to be everyone's respectable friend. He did not want a future as a dictator, only recognition for what he had already done, rewards in land for his troops, the ratification of the eastern borders he had drawn, and a new triumph that would be the greatest that anyone in Rome had ever seen. He also wanted a rest—and a new wife. The years when Mucia had boosted his reputation were long past; her own reputation for relationships with others had become an irritation during his absence and grounds for a homecoming divorce.

Crassus did not rest. He did not need a new wife, but he did want to frustrate Pompey's aims for primacy. The battlefields of Forum politics were much more favorable to him than those of Armenia, Cappadocia, and the Black Sea. As a counterweight to Pompey he began to advance further the prospects of Julius Caesar, who was planning to return from fighting in Spain and himself wanted the consulship. Crassus would be the one who bought it for him.

Pompey's concerns for his soldiers' rewards and his borders' ratification stayed at the top of the political agenda, but not in the straightforward way that he had hoped. He had hardly moved back into his great house on the Palatine Hill before Caesar's mother, Aurelia, and his wife, Pompeia, a granddaughter of Sulla, were the hosts of a sacred women's festival, the Bona Dea, at the official house of the absent Pontifex Maximus: Caesar's previous wife, Cornelia, the daughter of Cinna and mother of his only child, had died seven years before.

No men were allowed entry to this celebration of fertility and chastity in the presence of the Vestals. Not even Caesar himself would have been admitted had he been in Rome. But one man did get to see the sacred rites, Publius Clodius Pulcher, an aristocratic populist agitator, who had been trained as speaker in Crassus's own rhetorical school, backed as one of Crassus's many political insurance policies, and become Pompeia's lover, it was said.

The failure of Clodius's female clothing to disguise his identity was the first act in a farce whose plot slowly frustrated Pompey's ambitions. The borders of Syria and Judea, the extent of Deiotarus's rule in Galatia, and the freedoms of Philadelphia and the cities of the Jordan were all gradually wrapped within the trial of

Clodius for sacrilege. Old rivalries, family enmities, and jealousies over Pompey's generosity to his troops emerged day after day in a court open to cash and credit offers from all sides.

Caesar chose not to return from Spain and testify against Clodius, preferring to hold a favor for the future. Cicero destroyed Clodius's alibi for the night of the Bona Dea, creating an enmity that led to his own trial and exile for executing the followers of Catiline. Crassus paid the jurors the massive bribes required to exceed the bribes of others and assure Clodius's acquittal.

If money was not enough, sex with expensive boys and women were added to Crassus's offers. Cicero declared the jurors to be "a lower mob than ever sat at a gaming table," Crassus to be a balding whoremaster, and the few honest men on the jury panel to be like men terrified of contagion. The verdict was only narrowly in Clodius's favor despite this vast expenditure in cash and kind. Pompey fumed that the reasonable terms of his triumphant return were being neglected amid tales of cross-dressing, religious transgression, and the divorce of Caesar's wife on the grounds that, whoever was in that role, she should always be "beyond suspicion."

Crassus had to show Pompey his power without flaunting it. His protection of Clodius was a reminder to all his financial and political clients of what he could do for them — and what he could not do if they stood in his way. He had friends who had paid too much at auction for the right to tax the cities of Asia; they wanted his political help to renegotiate their contracts and protect the lands on which they had secured the loans to buy them. A major part of his power was that he could give that help.

But Pompey was now able to match him in bribes: a flood of land onto the market from bankrupt tax collectors might also help him provide farms for his retired troops. Crassus needed to be feared as well as to be a source of cash or credit. However amenable

Pompey seemed presently to be, it was sometimes useful to have that reputation as a wild bull with "hay on its horns" to warn the unwary. Crassus cultivated support among senators who were not his usual allies but who feared Pompey more. When Pompey tried to marry a daughter of Cato, perhaps the most important old-guard senator whom he needed for the smooth passage of his plans, Cato, to Crassus's satisfaction, declined the honor.

Crassus's backing of Caesar was always an even bigger investment. In return for help to the consulship, Caesar became Crassus's aide as much as ally, a relationship forgotten when the balance of power between them changed but important at the start. Cicero was less significant, but his showy new house on the Palatine was from the Crassus estate, bought at a price much less than it was worth: the two men shared, if rarely much mutual respect, an admiration for young Publius Crassus.

An immovable weight on Pompey's side of the political scales was his imminent triumph. Various factions in the Senate might block his rearrangement of Galatia and quibble over the land for his legionaries but could not block his third invitation to lead his troops and their plunder through the streets of Rome, a day, maybe two days, of celebration that would far outshine the one that had been reluctantly awarded to him by Sulla, erase the memory of the elephants trapped under the processional arch, and exceed any triumph by any general since the ritual had emerged from mist and myth some four hundred years before.

For the crowds packed for the triumph along the Sacred Way, the day before Pompey's forty-fifth birthday, September 61 BCE, was a chance to see exotic prisoners from all over the East, each in what was deemed their national dress, many carrying placards that told their previous status as princes, their future status to be prisoners, slaves, or free men, every verdict depending on the commander in the "red cloak of Alexander" at the center of the parade. The family of Mithradates of Pontus was there to remind Romans of the fifty thousand Italians whom the king had ordered killed in their Asian homes twenty-seven years before. On the side of carts were paintings of victorious battle scenes of revenge. There were ships' prows to show Pompey's suppression of the pirates. Former pirate kings marched alongside a former king of the Jews, Aristobulus, whose offer of a spectacular golden vine and an open gate to Jerusalem had not been enough to save him from the parade.

For senators considering the boundaries that Pompey had chosen for his conquered lands there were placards reminding of their names: Armenia, Pontus, Media, Colchis, Cappadocia, Paphlagonia, Syria, Cilicia, Judea, Palestine, each one a buffer between what was Roman and what belonged, probably but not certainly, to the Parthians. Pompey had thought the Parthians too weak and scattered to be worthy of a war. He had taken an interest in Parthian affairs but mostly by manipulating marriages. The daughter of Phraates of Parthia was in the parade because she was the wife of a troublesome prince of Armenia: her own daughter, Phraates' granddaughter, completed the humiliation of a country that was not even part of Pompey's conquest.

Within this great arc of territory were some nine hundred old cities, newly loyal to Rome, and forty cities newly founded, all payers of tax for the foreseeable future. There was Pompey's army, too, reconstituted for the occasion, a menacing reminder, each soldier with six years' pay, and a massive fortune, it was said, for each of some twenty officers.

For Crassus, and for anyone else concerned with the nature of money, there was the added sight of more money, in physical form, than anyone had ever seen: gold piled in heaps as though it were street dust, more gold in coins than the annual tax for the whole empire, gold on chariots, golden thrones and scepters, a moon of gold, the solid gold statue of Mithradates twice the size of the king who had killed himself, his own daughters, too, rather than join such a spectacle. There were fine objects, furniture, and jeweled rings that set an instant Roman fashion, thirty-three crowns of pearls, the most precious material of antiquity: but the story was of quantity not quality, enough treasure for weeks of triumph, too much alone being enough. This was what a central bank would have looked like if Rome had ever had such a bank to spur its business.

Aristotle had not been wholly wrong. While money could be made to work, to produce and reproduce just like an apple tree, that was not its primary purpose. Its very existence was its essence. The nature of money was in taking more than making. That was what the Romans did best.

When Crassus had been nine years old, a Roman general had found the greatest treasure trove of the age, in a temple at Tolosa in Gaul, some fifty thousand bars of gold that had been originally looted from the great Greek temple complex at Delphi. The general, it was said, had staged a bandit raid on his own money carts that were carrying the Tolosa treasure to Rome; he had taken foreign gold to meet his own sense of the public need just as Pompey was doing.

This had done him no good. As the story was told, like a warning to children, the gold had been cursed as it was being carried from Delphi. Anyone who touched it would die "a wretched and agonizing death." The Gauls had already discovered this and hoped that their own gods might rescue them. Upon the Romans it had brought fire from the North that only Marius, and all that followed from Marius's revolution, had been able to extinguish.

Money was not yet the god of the Roman world, but the gods

played a big part in banking it, their priests everywhere threatening raiders with revenge to discourage unjustified withdrawals. Pompey had raided many temples. In prime place on the triumphal parade was his staring head, molded in pearls, looking like Alexander the Great as Pompey had always liked to look. Crassus could not deny that Pompey was the richer man now, nor that Pompey had claimed a crown, too, for the virtue of clemency since, when the show was over, almost all the prisoners were sent back to their homes. Crassus could only hope that the gods might bring his rival down.

CHAPTER THIRTEEN

A Three-Headed Monster

Crassus and Pompey managed Caesar's election to the consulship for 59 BCE, the beginning of a phase for Crassus when it was even more than usually unclear whose side he was on and what the sides were. It was an unofficial pact, visible in various effects but secret in its workings. Within three years the "three-headed monster," in the words of a bold satirist, would be an open secret, the pact that would send Caesar to further glory in Gaul and Crassus to Parthia.

In its first form the monster delivered Pompey the ratification of his decisions in the East. The leaders of many cities had already declared a Pompeian Age, with Judea freed from its warring Jewish kings and incorporated into Roman Syria, Pontus freed from the family of Mithradates and merged with Roman Bithynia, and gains for Galatia in reward for the signal loyalty of its king, the Divine Bull. Pompey had long assured local rulers that he spoke and acted for Rome, and Rome had finally agreed that this was so.

Crassus won the renegotiation of the price that his friends, the *publicani*, had paid for the right to tax foreign citizens, including

Asian citizens, for using Asia's ports and other services. This was not a small matter. The publicani, who in many cases included Crassus himself, did most of the administrative work at Rome, bidding for such public responsibilities as feeding the sacred geese on the Capitol (the contract to the lowest bidder) and such public rights as the collection of specific taxes and duties (contract to the bidders, normally a group, who offered the most). The sums offered, agreed at public auction like the sales of the goods of the proscribed, were vast; tax contracts were hugely profitable unless the bidders made a bad mistake. Crassus's friends needed a renegotiation; the losing bidders were naturally not keen to help. Crassus could not help them by himself, but with Caesar as consul on his side, he could and did. Caesar also added a place for Crassus beside him in the college of priests.

Pompey married a new wife, Julius Caesar's seventeen-year-old daughter, Julia. This was an alliance between popular generals that alarmed traditionalists in the Senate much more than did the details of the Armenian border or the duty on olive oil into Cappadocia. Cato, who had refused Pompey his own daughter, was horrified at an outcome that for him was even worse. Cicero, too, made his hostility known, and when Clodius, still smarting from the Bona Dea trial, tried to exile him for his execution of Catiline's supporters four years before, no part of the three-headed monster came to Cicero's defense. Only Publius Crassus agitated for Cicero to stay in Rome and, when that plea had failed, to be quickly allowed to return. Pompey himself was delighted with his eastern settlement and his new wife, making less trouble for Crassus than at any time since his return from the East.

In Parthia political tumult was a wholly family affair. Phraates was under pressure from two ambitious sons, Mithridates and Orodes, and was surviving only because neither wanted the other to succeed. Mithridates, the elder, was claiming to have had some support from Pompey. Orodes was backed by the influential Surena family, who held a traditional right to be kingmakers. News from Parthia was always obscure, but the two brothers, while sufficiently cooperative to murder their father, could not agree to what happened next. After a short reign, even by recent Parthian standards, Mithridates was under arrest and Orodes was on the throne. This might or might not be interpreted as a snub to Pompey and to Rome.

The three-headed monster had more pressing concerns than the plottings within Parthia, not least its own future. Crassus, Pompey, and Caesar had disagreements of the kind that a secret deal could not reliably resolve. While not yet close to mutual murder, they were clashing in ways which made each of them afraid of the others.

Crassus had risen to a status closer to Pompey's but only by promoting his protégé, Caesar. Both Pompey and Crassus were nervous of Caesar's early successes in Gaul, the use that he had made of the legions that Crassus had helped to pay for, and the wealth and freedom for him that might soon follow. When the governor of the farthest part of Gaul unexpectedly died, Crassus failed to ensure that one of his own allies, Gaius Pomptinus, conveniently on the spot, should take over.

Caesar humiliated Pomptinus by ordering his friends in Rome to wear military black instead of celebratory white at ceremonies that the Senate had granted him for his modest successes. The message was clear that Gaul needed the serious leadership that only Caesar, not Crassus's man, could provide. Caesar was far from Rome but pulling the puppet strings more than Crassus could in the Forum, buying future support from far away. Skilled in communicating his victories, he was more present in the minds of

Roman voters than his colleagues mired in the mundane at home, in land distribution to retired soldiers and new regulation of personal debts.

Crassus and Pompey considered again creating a counterweight to Caesar's growing power by persuading the Senate to make Egypt a Roman province. This would be no easy task, but if Crassus were to be governor over the fields of the Nile, there would be no way that Caesar could exceed his wealth from the Rhone. Caesar was also taking huge bribes from the king of Egypt to keep him on his throne. All eyes were on Egypt, who should rule it and who should decide. A primary need for all was to protect their pliant royal ally in Egypt from his own family rivals who might either make the annexation harder or stop paying the bribes.

Any thought that Rome might take sides between the squabbling brothers of Parthia was removed by this higher priority. The governor of Syria had the nearest legions, and he could not be in two places at once. Aulus Gabinius, an ally of Pompey, was told to give up Mithridates and go to the aid of Ptolemy the Fluteplayer instead, a task that took him until Crassus was preparing for Parthia himself.

At home Pompey was not as popular as he had hoped. The euphoric mood of his triumph had faded. Crassus continued to give quiet backing to Clodius and other agitators for free food and other popular causes. Cicero, supported by both Crassus and his son, Publius, returned from exile, in August 57 BCE, seeking a greater closeness between Pompey and the Senate conservatives and thus a breach between Pompey and Caesar. Crassus was one of the first to greet Cicero at the Porta Capena, Rome's gateway to the South. When Caesar heard the news from Rome, it was increasingly of gang warfare, most of it between clients of his colleagues.

In the spring of 56 BCE Crassus was still focusing on the race to be first. Sensing that Caesar was falling behind and hoping to exploit the possibilities of that, he traveled to warn his former protégé of the latest threats to him from Pompey and Cicero. They met in the swamps of Ravenna, just north of the Rubicon River. For Caesar, who had been keeping troops for the winter in the safest part of his province, from where hostile Gauls had long been removed, this was about as far south as he could legally come during his governorship. For Crassus, who disliked being far from Rome in any circumstances, and was more used to having Caesar at his own door than visiting him, the setting was perhaps both the least bad it could be and well worth the inconvenience if it left Caesar further in his debt.

Before the fighting season in Gaul began again, Caesar invited both Pompey and Crassus to discuss their futures, this time to the somewhat drier town of Luca some 150 miles to the west. Luca was more convenient for the exchange of news and bribes between a general and his electors; some two hundred other senators also made the journey to hear of Caesar's hopes (and barely concealed expectation) of more time to complete his conquest, and his concern (vigorously expressed with his army all around him) that anyone be elected to the consulship for the following year who might summon him home.

After this it was clear, not only to Crassus and Pompey, but to everyone with a care for Roman politics, that the three-headed monster was more than a figment of satirical imagination. It was a pact. It was a fact. Pompey had once taunted Sulla, and irritated Crassus, with his boast that more men worship the rising than the setting sun. Caesar might now be rising, but his risks, too, were high. He needed allies as consuls in 55 BCE and would do what was necessary to have his will prevail.

Crassus was the most reluctant to admit this. It offended his honor to have to be consul because it suited Caesar: when asked whether he was a candidate, he persevered for months with the promise that he would do whatever was best for the republic. Pompey did not need or much want to be consul either. Rivals to all three dared to hope that they might win election and replace Caesar in Gaul with a lesser danger. Others, including Cicero, newly returned from his exile, were more realistic.

But Crassus, whatever his misgivings, was happy to be clearly acknowledged at the top table for three. Some senators boycotted meetings and wore mourning clothes to signal the death of the old order. Marcus Brutus, foreshadowing his leadership of Caesar's assassins a decade later, used his junior office at the Roman mint to produce a silver Liberty coin. Crassus's own extensive coin collection could not have avoided the young woman's face of Libertas, staring sternly at whoever might threaten her.

Brutus escaped, but more aggressive threats to the new order were cut down. Crassus sacrificed Clodius like the pawn that he was, a useful help in disrupting the Senate elite but necessary no more. Pompey reined in his own city dogs. Senatorial politics almost ceased. Both Crassus and Pompey became consuls, helped by some of Caesar's troops sent to dissuade dissenters at a delayed election. Their legislative agenda was the deal agreed at Luca.

Armies were for generals now. Whatever Marius had intended, by the time that Crassus was marching into Parthia and Julius Caesar through Gaul, their armies were highly conscious of who was paying them and for whom they were fighting. As a result of agreements at Ravenna and Luca, the command of Caesar in Gaul was extended for five years, the governorship of Spain remained with Pompey, although he was not obliged to go there, and Crassus was to be governor of Syria, from where he would be free to conquer an unknown country if he chose.

———

Caesar also agreed that Crassus should have his son, Publius, by his side for any Parthian campaign. This was a sacrifice that Crassus recognized and appreciated. Publius had no official position in Gaul, no rank beyond that of *adulescens,* a bright young man, but he had become something of a hero there. When Caesar believed that his war was almost won, he had put him in charge of the winter quarters on the west side of the new province. Publius had instead found an unexpected alliance of tribes that could normally be relied upon to be attacking each other.

In Caesar's absence Publius had to lead the Seventh Legion down the western coast from the north to the Pyrenees, facing guerrilla attacks from enemies reinforced by fighters from Spain with fresh experience of how the Romans liked to fight. The Seventh Legion was itself manned largely with Spanish troops. The resulting conflicts were reminiscent of the age of Publius's father and grandfather. More a dashing cavalry officer than a dour grinder down of infantry warfare, Publius was a risk-taking success, the kind of leader that Caesar most liked. At the same age his father had been more in exile than in command. His brother Marcus, also a newcomer to Caesar's staff, was beginning a long career of caution. Publius was different.

The story was told of how he came once close to disaster on the march south when drawn to follow enemy horsemen into a narrow valley. A mass of enemy infantry stood at the end of the trap. His own rapidly rising career, and Caesar's, too, was in the balance before he succeeded in escaping, finding the enemy's fortified camp, offering battle and then storming the rear gates. When the Gauls panicked, maybe fifty thousand of them it was said, Publius led a cavalry pursuit to a mass slaughter and surrender, giving Caesar control of the whole of western Gaul and a dramatic account for his war memoir, freeing himself to advance the interests of his father.

In January 55 BCE Publius returned to Rome. Caesar's version of Publius's own version of events followed soon. Crassus's hero son was considering a political career but had not yet taken the first steps. He was a very useful hero. With him were some of Caesar's soldiers to ensure that there was no impedance to the delayed election of Crassus and Pompey as consuls for that year. Intimidation was hardly needed when the day came for casting votes; there were no other candidates.

Publius gained a junior role as regulator of the Roman mint. He had a coin made with on one side Venus wearing a victor's laurel crown and on the other a rider beside a prancing horse, the first perhaps a homage to Caesar, who claimed the goddess as his ancestor, the second to the art of war that he himself, his name P. Crassus, beside the horse's head, most prized.

His marriage later that year was, in the view of his admirers, itself a prize. His wife was Cornelia Metella, in her late teens and already famed as an accomplished heiress to the Scipios, descendent of Scipio Africanus, defeater of Hannibal in 202. The family had recently excelled mainly in senatorial politics, and the link between her and the glamorous Publius had benefits for the future of both families. Cornelia's father was the grandson of Lucius Crassus, the orator and reformer whom Cicero most wanted Publius to emulate. Descent and family traits were the natural way at Rome of seeing character; everywhere there were high hopes for Crassus's cavalryman heir.

Publius himself, buoyed by his youthful triumphs in western Gaul, had matching ambition, in Cicero's view exceeding even that of his father to be the first man of Rome: Crassus's glamorous son wanted to emulate Cyrus and Alexander, the greatest cavalry commanders in history and the founders of enduring dynastic empires in the East, both of them gaining their greatest victories in their youth. Cicero's perception of his fellow Romans was ever sharp against excess; Publius was better than his father, but even the finest protégé who reached too far was, in Cicero's mind, a problem.

Before the end of 55 BCE Publius had also to make one last visit to Gaul. Crassus had persuaded Caesar not only to let his son accompany him to Syria after his consulship ended but to give him a thousand Gallic cavalry. Crassus and Pompey had ensured that this would not be at Caesar's personal expense: every part of the army in Gaul was now paid for by SPQR, all his decisions national decisions. Caesar did not need any longer to show that he was rich enough to finance his own legions.

In desert fighting the cavalry squadron from Gaul would be vital. Far from home, its loyalty would be assured. Publius returned north to collect his men and horses. His old Seventh Legion was already with Caesar in Britain, attempting to extend one end of the Roman Empire just as he and his father were about to do at the other.

CHAPTER FOURTEEN

How to Be First

Barely two miles of ancient wall ran between the Colline and Capena Gates, a ragged ribbon of stone blocks, ramparts, and ditches between the place where Crassus had won his first great victory to where he was beginning his campaign for a second, infinitely greater triumph. The highest, deepest fortifications toward the north recalled the years when Gauls were conquerors of Rome rather than its subjects; the southern sections, where Crassus was preparing his departure for Syria, were lower, a statement that there was no invader now for Rome to fear.

Behind the Capena Gate lay the tight bend of the Circus Maximus, the city racetrack where men and packhorses were awaiting their time to leave. Beyond were the first flat gray stones of the Appian Way, the road to Capua and on to the southern towns where he would gather his troops, recruiting where he could as once he had done for Sulla. He would be back among the Marsi at the stagnant Fucine Lake, listening to barely intelligible Latin, offering money for war, and ending in Brundisium, where lines of round-bottomed ships were ready for the voyage east.

The roadside crosses had long gone. The crucifixions of the men who fought with Spartacus were in a distant past. For its first few miles the Appian was lined only with the finest dead of Rome: the tomb of the Scipios, the new family of his son, would be one of the first sights that he would pass.

There were a few final details. Warfare, like business, was all about detail, about whom to trust and what the trustworthy should be promised in return. When the difficult decisions came, both fighting and finance were about reward, about money, and about making people feel good when they had no choice but to obey orders. The money by itself, in the strongboxes that followed his carriage, was always simpler than the politics surrounding it.

He had to calm his critics as best he could. One senator, who had slept in the Senate house to ensure he could object the next day, found himself locked in and barred from the Forum. Caesar had sent a supportive note. Pompey, more usefully, had provided some troops to show his commitment to his old rival's safe departure. Some of Pompey's veterans had come out of retirement for a last campaign.

Cicero was publicly supportive: Pompey and Caesar would not allow an open breach with him that might give encouragement to their enemies. At a dinner on the previous night the two men had talked. Cicero had chosen the setting, the famous riverside gardens of his daughter's husband's house. But there was no warmth between the host who sought power with words and the guest who preferred money. Their mutual suspicion remained. Cicero remained politely skeptical of Crassus's plans and wrote to a friend that Crassus had worn his general's cloak with nothing like the dignity of the last Roman conqueror of so great an age that he could recall. Crassus was a good-for-nothing compared to Aemilius Paullus a century before who, also in his early sixties, had brought to Rome the Macedonian treasure of Alexander's last heirs.

Further down the political ladders of Rome his business partners readily backed a plan that might give Rome control of the Silk Road to China. They gained, too, from Crassus's and Pompey's reforms of the juries in bribery trials, changes made on the principle that the rich were always less likely to be corrupted. The people's leaders suspected that, behind the fine principles, only Crassus and his friends would profit. The mood at the Capena Gate was raucous. Smoke and curses rose into the air. Wine mixed with incense whipped up a terror as though from the most ancient past.

Crassus was famed for disguising his intentions. No one knew exactly what the plan might be, merely the options from which Crassus would choose. He could threaten the Parthian king, taking hostages to ensure his future good behavior. Or, as Pompey had once considered, he could foment another Parthian civil war, supporting Orodes' brother, Mithridates, for the throne if Mithridates was still alive. Or he could choose conquest just as Caesar was choosing conquest in Gaul.

A dependent king could be a surer source of money than creating a province for Roman tax collectors to plunder: the Flute Player king of Egypt, gratefully being restored by Roman soldiers to his throne, was the latest beneficiary of such a judgment. A new Parthian province, however, would be a clearer achievement. The one might precede the other, but only a single decisive victory would be solely in Crassus's control. Some of the people's tribunes already thought that too much was in Crassus's control. Caesar and Pompey, whatever their outward shows of support, might come to feel the same.

Pompey knew how long Crassus's campaign would likely have

to be. He was confident in his own solid connections to the eastern kingdoms he had created. Caesar was happy to see Crassus threaten chaos to Pompey's eastern settlement — and if he failed, or was too old to last the course, his experience might help Caesar, after his conquest of Gaul, to follow and do better. The agreements at Luca and Ravenna were backed by a new law, promoted to the people's assembly by Gaius Trebonius, giving the provincial commands in Gaul, Spain, and Syria for five years without the need for annual renewal. But no one thought they would last that long.

Until Publius could join him, Crassus's closest confidant was Gaius Cassius, a restless officer in his early thirties, a supporter of Pompey, as his father had been. Crassus had already needed Trebonius for support in the Assembly; now he was dependent on Cassius, too. Both men would serve and then murder Caesar. This was the beginning of their careers.

At Brundisium Crassus was in a hurry. While his timetable for invading Parthia was relaxed (he had many options and could consider them as he wished), his opportunities for crossing the Adriatic were shrinking every day. Early November was outside the sailing season, and later was much worse. His heavy transport ships were already rocking in the bay, risking their safety, exhausting their crews, before the legions lined up to leave.

Skepticism about his campaign had followed him along the Appian Way. Potential troops had resisted recruitment. A seller of dried figs and dates was shouting to his buyers, "Cauneas! Cauneas!" advertising the origins of his fruit in the famed groves of Judea. His words were interpreted as "Cave ne eas! Cave ne eas!" "Beware! Don't go!" as reported to Cicero back in Rome.

The hardest soldiers had no choice but to become superstitious sailors, hundreds of them crammed belowdecks in each cavernous hull, knowing that before they had disembarked in northern Greece, let alone reached the date palms and fig trees of Syria, they would be fewer than had left Brundisium bay. The winds at sea were unusually strong, and many ships were lost, their cargoes' fates known only at the roll calls after landing.

Crassus, while counting out his soldiers, knew from letters carried on faster ships that his cause at home was no more popular than when he had left the Capena Gate. While Trebonius had been trying to pass the law for the next governorship of Syria, Crassus, normally calm and calculating, had hit a fellow senator who opposed his plan. Support had not improved since. He and Pompey had publicly spent their energy on laws to curb political street gangs and electoral bribery, but neither these measures themselves nor the irony of Crassus's part in them had deflected attention from the future for Parthia.

Cicero had to struggle hard, without recourse to violence, to stop the new consuls from curtailing the powers that their predecessors had granted. This was a not unusual hazard for Roman generals, but neither was it welcome. Crassus, used for so long to pulling the puppet strings of power, was now himself the puppet. He was dependent on Pompey to ensure that his mission was maintained and that their shared decisions still held, just as Cicero was depending on Pompey to control the ambitions of Crassus and Caesar.

CHAPTER FIFTEEN

A Divine Bull's Warning

After landing, Crassus led his legions through Macedonia, site of Aemilius Paullus's triumph as an old man, the achievement that, unbeknown to him, Cicero had so favorably compared to Crassus's own prospects. More than a hundred thousand from the villages through which he passed had been enslaved for Rome in Paullus's war. He then took his army to sea again, across the northern Aegean, before his final march to Syria through the borders that Pompey had defined in the past decade.

Galatia, a mountainous inland kingdom beneath the Black Sea, was one of the countries made significantly larger as a result of Pompey's mapmaking. The Galatians were originally Gauls who had settled in central Asia after their invasions three hundred years before. When they spoke, they still sounded like the men fighting Caesar for the forests of the Ardennes, a reminder that the Romans were merely the latest people – colonists, aggressors, whatever name was chosen – on the move through lands where others lived.

Crassus was well used to discussions about why Rome had come to exceed its rivals, past and present, and what was needed to make that superiority clearer still. This was a fashionable subject. Cicero was one of its masters. The answers were manifold. Its homeland was naturally the most fertile in the world. Under the soil there was obviously every possible precious metal because how could there not be? The genius of Rome was in not mining its wealth. Italy's gold and silver were able to feed its soil. Moreover, its people were prudent lawmakers, ingenious inventors, loved by the gods, and, perhaps most important, able to turn any deficiency into a self-deceiving advantage.

Deiotarus, Divine Bull of Galatia, had made his own country great by consistent flattering of the Romans and appreciation of their imperial sense of themselves. He ruled a large territory that had once belonged to a king who took a different view, Mithradates of Pontus, last seen as a twelve-foot golden statue in Pompey's triumph. Deiotarus owed much to Pompey. He had survived to be over fifty in a game where many died violently and younger.

When Crassus passed through Galatia, he found the king supervising the construction of a new city. He commented that it was perhaps a bit late in his life for such a project: "It's at the twelfth hour of the day that you are beginning to build." Deiotarus replied that Crassus, too, was leaving his biggest project rather late: "You yourself are not starting against the Parthians very early in the morning."

The Roman army, a straight line of legionaries and a ragged band of animals and supplies, marched on into Syria. Crassus's long life had been spent in planning, in grand strategy, tiny detail, and the most calibrated risk. Publius might provide the dash, but until he arrived, his father was proceeding step by step as he had always done. If Deiotarus knew what was good for him, he would keep his perceptions to himself.

Crassus was at the height of his power and hopes for more power. The first tycoon of Rome was ready to become its first man in every respect. He also knew that the legality of his campaign was complex, his support back home fragile at best. There needed to be nothing else out of order. The risks had to be mastered by the routine. As on the Palatine, so on the road to Parthia, his discipline was the same.

For every Roman soldier the camp was the world. Routine made a place Rome. The three same blasts on a bronze horn ordered the morning movement whether a legion was in Galatia or Gaul, the wetlands of Ravenna or the date groves of Judea. The first was for the packing of tents, the loosening of ropes, the lowering of poles, the rolling of a thousand sheets of soft leather. The second was for the loading of the baggage of war onto animals, the third the order to march, local scouts to the fore, the legionaries behind, cavalry to left and right.

Before every nightfall, officers rode ahead to choose the site for the next camp, marking out the bounds between Rome and the rest, streets with colored flags, the Cardo running north to south, the Decumanus east to west, each night the same streets, measured by the *metatores*. When the main mass of men arrived, the boundary became a ditch and a fence of stakes, not impassable, only a yard deep and across, but enough to mark what was Rome and what was not.

Crassus had his own tent, around it the tents of Cassius and his staff, within them trenches not as deep, filled with dry grass and reeds for a bed. Outside would be a platform, for the making of a speech, if that were necessary, and for the watching of birds to find good auguries, necessary always, whether the sky was full of desert vultures or night herons.

As far as possible away, at the bad end of the rows of rising tents, were the shithouses and the bread ovens. Every soldier knew his allotted place, the same letters and numbers every night, the same roof of leather from which next morning, at the sound of the horn, he would emerge again like a moth from a chrysalis.

Crassus's thirty-five thousand men were not the most experienced, but they included veterans who could inculcate the young. His officers were not from the heights of the aristocracy, but they represented the future as Crassus saw it, sons of newer senators, Publius's fellow *adulescentes,* men from the families who had helped him as an exile in Spain and covered his tracks against Catiline.

He had time to train his army for the time and terrain. If a legionary's tent was numbered AVII in Macedonia, it would be AVII by the River Balikh as it poured into the Euphrates: first left, second right, the Decumanus dividing the tenth cohort from the ninth, the Cardo, the north-south hinge. There was never a reason for a man to be lost. On the roads to Parthia there would be changes of place but no change of address. That was the start of everything, whatever the age of the man on the platform of command.

Once in Syria, certainty for the men was not matched by certainty for the man in the red cloak at their head. Crassus had choices about what preparations to make and for what sort of attack. He faced difficult decisions and conflicting advice. He could concentrate on diplomatic negotiations with Parthia's Armenian neighbor, aiming to use its troops to bolster his own and its hill territory to hide an invasion. Or he could aim to cross directly toward the Euphrates and the Tigris, hoping to provoke a battle on flat desert ground on which Romans excelled. In this case there would be less need for the Armenians, maybe no need at all.

Heavy dependence on Armenia would require trusting barbarian rulers who seemed to intermarry as often as they fought and whom individually he did not know, a course unattractive to his banker's mind. To fight from its territory would also risk further his legal status at home. Armenia was formally an ally of Rome, and it was not clear that Crassus had the authority, as governor of Syria, to use its neighbor as a launchpad for a war. Some thought he had no authority to start any war. Clarification of that point, even for a statesman long steeped in law, in using and circumventing it, would be as unattractive as it was probably impossible.

The direct approach, as soon as he had Publius and his cavalry, seemed to keep more of the decisions under his control. For once in his life, in an alien geographical and political landscape, the role of devious negotiator seemed a less desirable role than that of open warrior. Meanwhile, on the immediate eastern side of the Euphrates stood Greek cities that, while nominally owing loyalty to Parthia, did not owe it very much. The local Parthian governor, Silaces, had a small force that Crassus believed he could defeat with ease.

In the summer of 54 BCE he and his legions crossed the Euphrates. All went as well as he could have hoped. He found the local Parthian army, won a one-sided victory, and sent Silaces back to King Orodes with wounds as a clear message of his intent. He accepted the allegiance of Carrhae and three Greek cities by threats alone. He was even fortunate in disaster: the ruler of Zenodotium chose to massacre a force of a hundred Romans sent in to accept his surrender. Crassus sacked the town, house by house, sent all its inhabitants away as slaves, and gave his army a first sense of the cash that would be coming to them for their efforts.

After only a few months he had wounded a senior Parthian leader, sent a strong signal to Orodes, lost only a few dead and captured, hardened his army against the fierce desert heat, and replenished his treasury for the costs of the campaign so far. These were the tactics he knew best. His troops hailed him as Imperator, the title of Pompey and Caesar: this was a new experience on which he hoped to build.

CHAPTER SIXTEEN

Hairs on a Man's Palm

Back in Syria for the winter, father and son were reunited. Publius arrived as already a conqueror, bringing trophies of his victories in western Gaul, aristocratic friends from Rome, tales of his narrow escapes, and the thousand cavalrymen with their fast Gallic ponies, which would be needed for the following year. Publius was confident for the coming campaign. He had a personal historian, called Apollonius, who would chronicle his successes. For Crassus this was the last piece in his personal and political future.

Among the officers who had returned from the Euphrates there was a greater concern. Their victories had seemed suspiciously easy. They had heard rumors within the Greek towns that the Parthians had arrows which could penetrate the thickest Roman armor. Nothing like that had been seen in their profitable summer campaign. The Parthians knew more about the Roman way of warfare than the Romans knew of theirs. It was almost as though they had been testing their invaders, lulling them into complacency.

Gaius Cassius, sensitive and suspicious throughout his life, felt that his advice was going unheeded. Instead of training the troops in the light of the latest intelligence, Crassus was counting his money, sending out temple raiders so that he should have more to count. When he should have been holding competitive exercises to test endurance and tactics, he was weighing the treasures from the spa town of Hierapolis and working out how much each local council should pay. Sometimes Crassus would assess exactly what was owed, then graciously decline to accept it, a practice better suited to banking for politicians in Rome than to winning a war. Cassius was keeping a diary for a future memoir; that was just one of the lessons that he had learned from Caesar.

According to Plutarch, a temple priest himself who liked reporting the dissatisfaction of the gods, there was a winter day when the triumphant Publius Crassus tripped at the gate of a Syrian goddess, an alien version of Venus, one who governed moisture, seeds, and the origins of life. Crassus himself, following immediately behind, then fell over his son. Publius could be seen as riding for a fall in every sense. Plutarch, as later readers clearly saw, had good access to the memoir of Gaius Cassius.

At the beginning of spring an embassy arrived from Armenia with six thousand cavalry and the offer of further forces if Crassus would make his main invasion of Parthia by the northern route through the Armenian hills rather than directly across the Euphrates. On higher, rougher ground, the Armenians advised, there would be less advantage for the enemy horsemen.

Crassus saw more potential traps in this than advantage. He took some notice of the kings of much smaller territories. Abgar of Osrhoene had come to him with scouts who knew the local terrain. He had also offered soldiers whose services Crassus had gratefully refused and cash which he had gratefully accepted. Abgar became an almost trusted adviser.

The Parthian king also sent ambassadors, a group of distinguished elders led by a man called Vagises, bearded and trousered
like the images on his coins, with an offer for Crassus to consider.
Vagises asked Crassus why he was making unprovoked war against
a people who had given him no cause. He noted that if Crassus was
a genuine representative of the Roman people, there would be war
without end, but if, as they had been told, he was a mere private
adventurer, out for prestige and profit, the great Orodes would be
magnanimous, respectful of his invader's old age, and bid him fare-
well. The prisoners they had taken could go home, too.

Crassus saw this as just another bit of barbarian bombast. He
replied that he would give his answer when he was in the royal city
of Seleuceia, where Orodes' deposed brother, Mithridates, was a
prisoner. Vagises held out a soft hand, palm upward, laughed, and
said: "Hair will grow here, Crassus, before you see Seleuceia."

This was a local Parthian insult behind one that was clear to
anyone. Crassus's lessons in language and rhetoric would have introduced him at an early age, to the *adunaton*, the Greek word for
saying that something cannot happen until something impossible
happens, deserts freezing over or dogs climbing pear trees. Hair
cannot grow on the palm side of even the hairiest hand; thus Crassus would never see the capital of Parthia in the West.

Crassus may not have understood the hidden meaning, nor
may Plutarch, who told the story in Crassus's Life. For a follower
of the prophet Zoroaster, a man with hair on his palms was a met-
aphor for a masturbator; spilling seed without purpose was a sin
of the degenerate and the ill-disciplined. The sophisticated emissary of the Parthian king would have to become the lowest of the
low before Crassus came to Seleuceia, and that was absolutely not
going to happen.

The Parthians had by this time become contemptuously amused

by the erotica found in the possessions of their Roman prisoners. Sexual adventures from the Ionian city of Miletus were particularly popular. In the world of the Parthian ambassador, princes on campaign had carriages of slave women to meet their needs; their soldiers were themselves slaves whose behavior hardly mattered. Anything else was mildly barbaric.

The ambassadors returned to their king. Crassus learned at the same time that he could expect nothing from Armenia: it was just as well that his expectations were already low. Orodes was himself sending an army against Armenia; he did not seem afraid to fight on two fronts. The Roman invasion was maybe a mere irritant in the region. The real quarrel was the permanent dispute between neighbors. Or maybe the Parthians' Armenian invasion, like their prophecies of hairy palms, was just barbarian posturing. Crassus did not care. He was resolved to fight on his own terms, with Publius at his side, as he had intended since last seeing Caesar at Luca. Even Cassius, uncertain as he had become about his commander's tactics, could hardly expect a Roman general to retreat after the smears of abuse he had just received.

CHAPTER SEVENTEEN

Camels and Bows

Crassus had not yet seen the adversary whom Orodes had sent to block his path. He had not even a picture of Surenas, the title of the young aristocrat from the sprawling Parthian east, who, unless he were himself to become king, would never have his face on any coins. It was said to be a fine, somewhat effeminate face, nothing like the grizzled, warty features of Orodes and his many recent predecessors, nothing like his own old man's face either, as Deiotarus had impudently made clear.

Surenas was rumored to be rich, with hundreds of square miles of Parthia to his name and thousands of slaves from whom he could pick his horsemen. But, while younger, he could hardly be richer than Crassus. Of that, at least, Crassus could feel sure. Parthia was a land of many private armies. A Roman general might once have noted that and claimed confident superiority for the public armies of Rome. In the age of Caesar, Pompey, and Crassus that was not a distinction any longer easily made.

Nor did Crassus know much about what sort of army Surenas led. It was hard to put together a picture from the observations of local scouts and spies. Accounts of wheeling pony riders armed with tiny bows were commonplace; so, too, were tales of camel trains and of the cataphracts, huge, unwieldy horses and riders, armored like elephants and liable to be no more useful than his fabled beasts had been for Hannibal.

Except for the cataphracts, aristocrats such as himself, and the camel drivers (status unknown), Surenas's force was almost wholly slaves, most of them born on his own lands. The freeing of the enslaved was unknown in Parthia, purchase of new slaves less necessary than in Rome. This was probably an advantage in loyalty over using Armenians, but nothing like as good as having free Romans in the field. The Parthian army was also very small, about a quarter the size of Crassus's force, or at least no one had reported any massed infantry of the kind that was necessary to win any serious battle. Maybe it was on its way to fight Armenians.

This did not mean that Surenas necessarily had no fighters on the ground. They could be kept hidden so as to deceive. Caesar was the master of such deception, and the sand dunes beyond the Euphrates were more suitable for concealment even than the forests of Gaul. The scouts' reports could also themselves be a deception, given deliberately to confound his plans. It was safer to trust nothing and no one.

In Crassus's experience, and that of Pompey and Sulla in the East, the outcome of battle always depended on infantry in the end. Disciplined lines of Roman legionaries, shield to shield, each man defending the sword arm of his neighbor, were almost never bettered. Cavalry would harass, preen, and swirl, but once their arrows were fired and their spears thrown, they would be crushed by any well-trained Roman legion, a truth recognized from the tin mines of Spain to the temple treasuries of the Black Sea. The difficulty, as in his war against Spartacus's slave army, would be in finding his enemy, not in defeating it.

Gaius Cassius and some of the army's other officers were alarmed by new reports of Surenas at the Greek towns that Crassus had garrisoned and assessed for tax in the previous year. The worry was not so much that his forces might have occupied the towns (no one had ever described a Parthian siege of anywhere) but what the effect of their weapons would be on the Romans guarding the walls. Reliable eyewitnesses, it was said, had seen strange missiles fired from far out of sight, striking with extraordinary force. The cataphracts, far from being cumbersome elephants, were armed with spears that nothing could resist and shielding plates, on every part of their body, that nothing could break through.

Crassus considered such continuing talk a deliberate assault on his men's morale. He had promised Pompey's veterans easy victories and easy money of the kind that they and their predecessors had won before against Cappadocians, Armenians, and other soft targets of the East. He did not want to explain high-velocity missiles and equine tanks: the stories had surely to be like the tall tales beloved by all travelers, exotica exaggerated by too much time on the road.

Army priests who took the regular auguries outside his tent, who observed the pecking of birdseed and the entrails of sheep, could normally be relied upon to tell a commander what he wanted to hear. To Crassus's frustration the latest messages to him from the gods, as well as from his officers, were not predicting great victory. When his traveling prophets placed the final sacrificial stomach organs in his hands, the ritual act of purification before departure, Crassus dropped the blooded mess to the ground. He recovered well, smiling, blaming old age, promising that no weapon would ever fall in the same way. But those around him were appalled.

Undaunted, he and Publius, with Cassius prominent among those recording their dissatisfaction, led their men back across the Euphrates. It was April 53 BCE. Summer heat was just beginning to rise from the river. The legions marched in full armor, ever ready to fight, their seven bronze eagles held high, keeping as close as possible to the bank in order to prevent encirclement if Surenas chose to attack rather than hide. That seemed unlikely, but success came always to Crassus from the minimizing of risk.

Their aim was to meet Surenas or reach Seleuceia, whichever came first. Crassus had the pleasant prospect of seeing hair grow on the palm of Orodes' ambassador. He had no interest any longer, it seemed, of replacing Orodes with his brother, the outcome that Pompey had wanted, Rome's *casus belli* whenever anyone had wanted one. Mithridates III had died in prison, a family event not likely to have been an accident.

The war was becoming ever simpler. Messengers confirmed that Orodes himself was deep into his punitive raid on Armenia. Whether this was a genuine attack or a feint to deceive Crassus hardly mattered. Future diplomacy, after he had defeated Surenas, might require his own temporary Armenian alliance to defeat Orodes. In the meantime there was only one adversary to find and no neighborhood entanglements to bind him in their knots.

The composite bow of the Parthians was not a secret weapon. Men on the distant flatlands of the roads to China had long known how to raise an arrow's range and power by using different materials in different parts of the bow from which it was fired, bone on the side close to the archer, animal sinews on the opposite side, snake skin against excess dryness or damp, varied kinds of wood glued together by trial and error until the rules for the perfect weapon were clear. The Romans knew the process, too, but the mass manufacture of composite bows was complex and expensive: one formula meant more power, another more accuracy, one suited river air, another the desert. Arrows, too, were of different kinds, heavy and light, armor-piercing and showering from the air like rain.

The Parthians had chosen to master these minutiae that meant so much; the Romans, relying mainly on foreigners for their archers, had not. Surenas's horsemen, circling in dusty wheels inland from the riverbank, had spent much of their youth balancing horse, rider, and bow to create the most explosive force: the skill brought them their food from high-flying birds and distant desert beasts, also their privileged place in their master's army. Publius's cavalry, riding either side of Crassus's columns, carried similar weapons, but perhaps better attuned for Aquitania. Legionaries did not fire arrows at all, a technique of warfare that in the Roman military rule book could be only temporary, a brief irritant, until both sides' quivers were empty and the real business of infantry war could begin.

Crassus was not an easy man to advise. Some of his entourage urged caution, the building of a fortified camp on the riverbank, a more permanent base in enemy territory than the town of tents that the legionaries routinely erected every night, a port for supply and a place of greater safety. Others thought that Surenas had already had too much time to prepare and should be hunted like desert prey without delay. That kind of dispute was common enough on campaign; it was nothing that would have surprised Sulla, Pompey, or Caesar, mentors and rivals whose advice, however, was not available to Crassus.

Publius, his son, and Cassius, his senior officer, tended toward opposing views. Cassius was more cautious, both as a soldier and as a student of politics. He was a writer and a thinker, naturally skeptical, both about excessive concentration of power and dynastic ambitions. His family's first consul, Cassius Viscellinus, five hundred years before, had been an early populist, put to death for giving land to the poor and trying to make himself a king. Viscellinus's was a lesson learned and still felt. Cassius supported Pompey for fear of someone worse.

Crassus was prey to both positions. He worried that the cautious were driven by baseless fear; those reporting unstoppable giant knights and arrows that ripped through shields had succeeded in more than good storytelling. The confident, by contrast, were perhaps impatient. Publius was impatient, a vice of which Crassus himself had never been accused and whose absence had long served him well.

He had few local advisers. One was still Abgar, from Osrhoene to the north, who had served Pompey. Abgar had information that others did not. He said that the Parthian army was nearby, watching the Romans pass, and could easily be found and overwhelmed if Crassus were to overrule the fearful and turn inland.

Agbar showed the way. The Romans watched the green turn gradually to gray, grasses to sand. The legionaries began to complain. They were not ready for such terrain. Agbar reminded them roughly that they were not in Campania (which men who had marched with Crassus to Brundisium did not need to be told) but in Arabia (which was not strictly true). The grumbling continued for a day and night until suddenly Agbar and his scouts disappeared.

Crassus did not know why his guide had gone. He sent his scouts ahead to find out. Maybe Agbar was checking that Surenas and his archers were where he was expecting them to be. Maybe he was withdrawing so as to be better able to join the winning side if a battle took place. He might be betraying Crassus or hedging his bets. No one knew.

Any questions about Agbar's whereabouts and motivation quickly faded when many fewer scouts returned than had left. Surenas and his cavalry were closer than Crassus, even in his greatest enthusiasm for close conflict, had expected. Publius and Cassius arranged the legions into an advancing square, a formation that was a standard feature of Marius's army reforms when Crassus was still a boy. Publius took one side, Cassius the other. Crassus stood behind the center, his legionary eagles raised high, the Gallic cavalry spread so as to protect all fronts. There were no reports of Parthian infantry, only of giant cataphracts, armored from rider's helmet to horse's hoof, archers on tiny ponies, and a long line of twin-humped camels, like a moving castellated wall, in the dust of the near horizon.

The camel was no more a secret weapon of war than was the composite bow. Aristotle had explained the two different types, the single-humped dromedary from Arabia and its twin-humped, soft-bearded cousin from Bactria on Parthia's ragged eastern frontier. Roman armies had faced enemies on camels, sometimes a cross-breed of Bactrian and Arabian, more than a hundred years before. Mithradates of Pontus had used them against Pompey. Camels had height and endurance; they carried heavy loads for days without water or food; they also terrified horses unless the horses were especially trained. For a Roman general in the East they had always been exotic and never very important.

But Surenas's army, when it first came into Crassus's sight on the road to Carrhae, showed no signs of being a camel corps. It hardly seemed a corps at all, more a swirling cloud of hooves driven by a tom-tom of drums, strong only in sound and smoke. The only discernible discipline was within the line of cataphracts, their vast weight of armor vainly disguised in animal skins, vulnerable, in Roman eyes, to the force of any legionary assault as long as the legions could get close. There was no heavy infantry. There were camels but only far away.

The cataphracts charged, stripping off their disguises to reveal shining scales of steel, hoping to intimidate, stabbing down with the long spears tied to their saddles. The Roman line held firm, locking shield to shield in the iron wall that in Crassus's lifetime had held off far more serious adversaries in Italy, Gaul, Spain, and by the Black Sea. It was almost a token attack, the giant figures seeming more theatrical than threatening, quickly dividing down each side of the square, the archers on their ponies following behind.

The Romans were surrounded but, by their own rules of war, still impregnable. Crassus ordered a cavalry charge against the enemy archers. After a short exchange, Caesar's best horsemen from Gaul were in retreat. The ferocious Parthian arrow fire delivered devastating penetration that the legionaries could see for themselves when the men and their mounts were back within the square. But according to the wisdom of convention, it could not last. Archery assaults lasted only as long as the archers had arrows. That was what the tacticians taught. That much Crassus knew.

Surenas had some nine thousand mounted bowmen. It was an unbalanced force by normal calculations, one perhaps forced upon him by Orodes' need for infantry against Armenia. Or maybe he had a youthful openness to a new idea. Whether enforced or not, the mass of Parthian archers began quickly to make a massive impact. Dipping and wheeling on the backs of ponies without saddle or stirrup, they fired arrows in sheets and clouds, straight into the legionary wall like battering rams, arced into the air to fall as deadly rain.

The archers did not need to be accurate, only unrelenting. When Crassus sent cavalry in pursuit, they retreated, twisting their bodies, firing as they fell back, the maneuver that lived on in the memory of the legionaries as a unique amalgam of retreat with honor and, in wider memories, as "the Parthian shot."

As each rider returned to the fray, he passed Surenas's line of camels loaded with fresh arrows. The rank smell meant nothing to the horses trained on the same faraway estates. The reloading made possible an assault that within the Roman square seemed without end. The composite bows were constructed for force, the arrows barbed to stay inside a wound, but neither the bows nor the arrows were as much of an innovation as the thousand camels, in a long line flowing to the Carrhae battlefield from the desert dust.

Crassus needed time to reassess. That could be gained only by driving the archers from at least one side of his beleaguered army. He ordered Publius to gather his Gauls and get close to their tormenters. On the western edge of Gaul Publius had taken risks and been lucky. He had been distrustful of forces that were not part of his legion. He had concentrated their efforts, not on fighting, but on keeping up the supply of slingstones and rocks. On the western edges of Parthia he had to trust his Gauls against an enemy as mobile and as thoughtful about ammunition supply as he had been himself. Publius heard his father's order and needed no more encouragement to seize again the hero's role. Flanked by two of his old friends from Rome, would-be leaders of the next generation, he reacted with the speed that Caesar would have approved in Aquitania, but with the frenzy, perhaps, of a man too long compelled to patience.

The square opened so that Publius and his fellow officers could advance, corralling Caesar's one thousand cavalrymen behind them. Four thousand legionaries followed. The Parthians turned and fell back toward their cataphracts. Perhaps they were surprised. Perhaps they were obeying orders. Certainly Surenas knew that his men (and they absolutely were his men) were never so dangerous as when in retreat. The archers joined the cataphracts, and the two great forces of this Parthian army turned again to attack Publius and his lightly armed Gauls, the cataphracts to the fore, the bowmen behind.

The Parthians surged and kept on surging. It was the continuity of the assault, more than the assaults themselves, that again shocked the Romans. Publius and his men no longer had the momentum of their charge. They were isolated from the main Roman force, cut off in what looked from this point like not a relief effort but a classic trap.

Publius himself took an arrow wound on his hand. He could no longer hold a sword. His Gauls fought on furiously as though Caesar himself were still their commander. They tore at the long spears of the cataphracts, jumping to the ground and stabbing at the less protected bellies of their cumbersome mounts. The forces were balanced in number, but the weight of force favored the Parthians. Publius and his men were surrounded just as they had been surrounded before. They had no defense against the arrow clouds and no line of retreat.

Crassus, barely a few flat miles into the country he intended to conquer, was still inside the square that Publius's breakout had been intended to relieve. He could not see the coming catastrophe. He ordered a move to slightly higher ground from where he could be a little safer but still offer no support to the bravery of Publius and his Gauls. Crassus could not, for the sake of his son, risk his entire army with a counterattack. He had to pause, regroup, reassess. He was losing a battle of equipment, preparation, and supply, all the dull necessities of war in which he saw himself as the master.

Publius could no longer fight. He still had the Parthian arrow through his hand. He struggled to the top of a small patch of raised ground, ordering those of his legionaries who could still hold a shield to form a small circle around the horses and the wounded, a miniature replica of the horror happening on a grander scale less than a mile away. The thousand men whom Publius had led as a hero through Europe and Asia retreated, with no sort of Parthian shots, to whatever greater safety lay behind the thin legionary line.

Surenas's archers continued to fill their quivers from the camel paniers. The shaggy-bearded Bactrians swayed and grunted. The arrows slammed and fell with even greater intensity in the circle of five thousand men than they did in the square of thirty thousand. Publius was too wounded to be able to help. He did not want to hinder. His line was almost certain to collapse. His father had no further cavalry to deploy.

Publius was determined not to be marched in any version of the triumph that the Parthians might use. Like his grandfather, he refused to see his enemy victorious. A brave death, as his mentor, Cicero, argued, would eradicate the memory of even the most incompetent failure. He ordered a soldier to drive a sword through his side. One of his student friends from Rome followed his lead; another had the strength to kill himself, and one by one every other officer followed as best they could.

The cataphracts delivered the final deaths, lumbering up the shallow incline and spearing the helpless Gauls as though they were in a Roman arena before a highly contested election, each candidate for office competing to put on the bloodiest show. The Parthians took around five hundred Romans and Gauls as prisoners, for their victory parade and for the mercy of Orodes. Surenas ordered Publius's head to be severed, stuck on a spear, and carried from the circle to the square.

Crassus had already sent scouts and messengers for news of Publius and his men. The first never returned. The second reported the news of imminent disaster but not yet the latest news of Publius's death. Crassus broke his square and, risking his legions too late for the sake of his son, moved toward the circle. It was not long before he learned that the risk was futile. The sounds of war had fallen silent; only the tom-tom drums of victory sounded over the sand. The camels had gone. A cataphract, its rider as unidentifiable as his horse, held up his trophy on a spear as though it were a legionary eagle. Crassus saw his son for the last time as he had last seen his own father, not in the Forum but in a faraway desert, iron in his skull, neck circled in blood, dead eyes fixed in a sightless stare.

CHAPTER EIGHTEEN

A Brawl over a Horse

The day was not yet over. Nor was the war necessarily yet lost. If Crassus could begin to lead his survivors back to the Euphrates, he had a chance to stop in friendly territory, reinforce, and return to Syria for a second invasion in the following year. He had not come far; he did not have far to retreat. He had lost a skirmish. That was all. The death of Publius was a personal tragedy, no more than that. If he reorganized his army with new cavalry, in the numbers required to counter the tactics of Surenas, he could still win his triumph. Great victories would obliterate small defeats as they always had, in Pompey's and Caesar's reports to the Senate, and in the future histories of all three of them that would follow.

The author of one of those histories, Plutarch the priest of the Delphic oracle, heard various reports of how Crassus, the banker on the battlefield, tried to turn loss to gain. While Surenas prepared for a fresh assault, his battered opponent made a speech to his troops, still some twenty thousand, some at least still strong. While the sorrow at the loss of Publius was his alone, Crassus said, he asked for any pity that the legionaries felt to be turned to rage against the enemy. He reminded them of how the Scipios, the family of Publius's widow, had turned disasters to triumphs in the past, one of them against the heirs of Alexander the Great in this very territory where Parthians now ruled; Romans were favored by Fortune, but more than that, they were strengthened by losses and the courage of those who had risked their lives for their city.

These were fine words, but the losses continued. Surenas applied the same brutal tactics as those of the morning. At the very end of the day he sent a message to Crassus offering one night to mourn his son before he could either be taken to Orodes to surrender or be carried there as a dead man. Surenas needed Crassus dead or alive to be sure that the Romans did not return, stronger and wiser, in the following year. The attacks did not cease until night fell over the desert.

The Parthians made camp close by. They did not seem to want to fight at night. Crassus decided to answer Surenas's message by taking such advantage as he could from what seemed his one opportunity to escape. If he took only the able-bodied, he had a chance to reach Carrhae by dawn; if he marched at the pace of the wounded, he would not. The "courage of those who had risked their lives," some four thousand men, had to be merely a figure of speech. As Crassus led out his men, the sound of screams and groans from the abandoned only slowly faded behind them.

Those on the march could not be certain that the Parthians would hold back from attacking at night. It only seemed that this was so. Crassus did not risk the straightest route to Carrhae. He formed his men into battle lines and reformed them for marching. He did it again. He changed his course to evade men who never came, who were sleeping after a great day in their martial history even if their master might not yet have told them how great it was.

As many Romans died on the cold night retreat as in the battles themselves. The line stopped and started and stopped again. The remains of the Gallic cavalry were the first to approach the walls of Carrhae. When they arrived, their leader did not identify himself, or give any but the briefest news that there had been a clash between Crassus and the Parthians, before riding off again to Roman Syria. Caesar's Gauls had had enough. The garrison commander sent out a search party which, without their help, found Crassus and the bulk of his army, a force now crumbled to some fifteen thousand men.

Surenas was still following, delayed first by ordering a massacre of the Roman wounded who had been left behind, second by mopping up stragglers who could not keep up with Crassus's retreat, and third by not knowing precisely where Crassus was and where he was heading – to Carrhae or directly to the border with his cavalry. Surenas's uncertainty was at that point Crassus's greatest strength, an advantage as quickly destroyed as others he had squandered.

Surenas sent an emissary to Carrhae offering a peace conference with Crassus. The Romans should have refused to talk. Instead Gaius Cassius accepted the offer, thus giving Surenas the vital information that he needed: Crassus was inside the town and not with any other of the divided Roman forces. The Parthian cataphracts and archers began crowding against the city walls.

This was not a besieging force. The Parthians had neither the equipment nor the experience to surround a city and break its walls. But Crassus still had vastly the bigger army, much the bigger problem of supply, and no certainty of where relief might come from the outside. As soon as Crassus realized Cassius's error, he had no option but to do what Surenas feared he was already doing, to split his troops into separate bands, one led by Cassius, one by himself, others by junior leaders of his shattered officer corps, each one to break out and find its own way to safety through the desert night.

Surenas had the single aim of finding Crassus. In case his prey was in disguise, he took Roman prisoners whom, if necessary, he could torture to identify their commander. Whether Cassius or any other Romans returned to Syria was of no comparable consequence to him. This was Crassus's war, fought for Crassus's purposes alone (that is what he and Orodes had long understood), and without him it would stop.

There were many possible nighttime pathways back to the Euphrates. Crassus did not find the best of them. As he came closer to the river, the land became greener and wetter. The terrain that his legionaries had so recently complained of leaving was now taking some of them back—not, however, into fertile fields, but into quagmire and marsh. When the pink desert dawn came, his men were as vulnerable to their hunters as a flock of ducks. Surenas was closing in for the kill.

Crassus's last piece of good luck was that another fleeing Roman party was on higher ground, where its scouts could see the inevitable conclusion. Several thousand demoralized soldiers descended into the marsh and led their commander and his men back to their somewhat safer camp. Surenas did not pursue them onto terrain much less favorable for his cavalry than the plain below. He sent a message with an offer from Orodes of a truce.

Crassus was suspicious. His long life had prepared him to be suspicious of any negotiating position so weighted in his own favor. He could not know whether Surenas was himself behind the king's offer or whether Orodes, jealous maybe of Surenas's success and anxious for his own position, had overruled his glamorous sub-ordinate. Reliable news of Parthian politics was wholly lacking.

There had always been Romans who pretended to know. De-feat at Carrhae had emboldened those among his officers, and their men, who felt that the king had his own good reasons for clem-ency. Since he had surely to want no further invasion, he might think that Rome's humiliation had already been enough. Crassus faced a mutiny from angry men who had experienced nothing in Parthia but arrow wounds and exhaustion; they had little faith in their commander's ability to lead them to safety. From the next marsh there would be no rescue. No one had seen the group led by Cassius since their ragged departure from Carrhae.

Crassus agreed to meet Surenas. He sent representatives ahead to agree the terms of the talks. None returned. With a small escort of officers he continued his descent to the plain. Surenas and his own guard were on horseback. Crassus and his party were on foot. Immediately behind Surenas were two grooms with a riderless horse. The Parthian kingmaker, little more than a third the age of Crassus, offered a mount to the older man before him.

Crassus could hardly refuse. When he took his seat, a groom slapped the horse's flanks and urged it to gallop back to the camp of cataphracts and archers. Two of his escorts tried to grab the reins. One of them killed one of the grooms and was then himself killed by the second groom. In what was hardly more than a brawl over a horse, Marcus Licinius Crassus, one of the world's wealthiest men, was the last to die.

Surenas ordered his head and hands to be severed and sent to Orodes. The Parthian king might have preferred Crassus alive, but there was to be no doubting his identity in death. Surenas offered peace terms to the Roman survivors and took enough new prison-ers to make his triumph clear. One of these, Gaius Paccianus, from the family who had helped Crassus in Spain, also looked very like Crassus. Or that was how he seemed to Surenas. Or maybe that was an illusion. It was often hard to distinguish one invader's face from another. At the perilous court of King Orodes, it was best that there be no possible misunderstanding. He ordered the pursuit and massacre of all the rest who could be found.

CHAPTER NINETEEN

Crassus's Triumph

The prophecy of the Parthian ambassador in the previous year had proved correct. Crassus never reached Seleuceia; only his severed head and hands did. Vagises had said that there would be hairs on his open palm before Crassus arrived at Orodes' western capital, an impossibility, he jibed, since he, unlike the barbaric Romans, was no masturbating ape. After Carrhae the palm of Vagises was still proudly without hairs. When the courtiers of the king wanted to mock the sexual preferences of their invaders, they now had more of the contents of their prisoners' baggage, numerous copies of the Milesiaca, famed Greek erotica for travelers far from home. The Parthians found this very amusing.

The man tasked with delivering Crassus's head to Orodes was the local governor, Silaces, who had lost the first battle of the campaign beside the Euphrates. Then Crassus had been hailed as Imperator after easily scattering the cavalry of Silaces. For being forced to skulk back wounded from defeat and giving the enemy valuable false encouragement, Silaces was given the honor of bringing back the good news. When historians began to write the story of Crassus's catastrophe, this was another kind of Parthian shot. Some added that his open mouth, shriveled by desert air, had been filled with molten gold as testament to his lifetime of greed, and that when Silaces brought the king his gift, the barbarian court was watching a performance of Euripides' last tragedy, *The Bacchae,* and that Crassus's head became a stage prop for the end of the show.

The Bacchae was not a play that Crassus had likely ever seen. It is not known to have ever been performed in Rome. Its protagonist is Pentheus, a stubborn Greek king who refuses to accept the superiority of the eastern god Dionysus. Pentheus thinks he can move mountains. He sees two suns in the sky. He feels like a god himself, and his punishment is to be torn apart, decapitated by maddened Dionysiac worshippers led by his own mother, who thinks that the head on her spike is that of a mountain lion.

If it were true that Crassus's head was substituted for that of Pentheus in the Parthian production, both the choice of play and the timing of Silaces' arrival showed impressive theatrical invention. Crassus would have starred in a play whose performance he had never watched, whose themes he had never thought of. By the time that accounts of Carrhae were spreading throughout the Roman world, the story of the head was so good that it did not need to be true.

Seleuceia was the old Greek part of a sprawling urban landscape that continued to Ctesiphon, the new city that the Parthians had built for themselves, gluing their own ways of life and thought onto those of the people they had supplanted. Followers of Zoroaster and Aristotle met on the roads between the two; so did those who followed only carts and camels. They knew of the Romans' love of a triumph; they decided on a triumph of their own.

In this victory parade the figure of Crassus played a further role that did not invalidate the prophecy of Vagises. Although Surenas lacked a living Crassus to put on show, he had the prisoner Paccianus, who looked like Crassus and whom he could dress like a great Roman lady, hoist upon a cart, and deliver humiliation on hardly less great a scale. Paccianus had known Crassus all his life; his family had welcomed him on his Spanish exile. Even many a Roman might have been deceived by Paccianus playing Crassus in drag along a dusty street; to the subjects of the Parthian king, he was as close to the real Crassus as political theater could ever demand.

If Surenas had wanted to understand more about the character of his enemy, a talk with Paccianus would once have been a good way to start. But he had no need for that now. Crassus was just a character, a man in woman's clothing, an object to ridicule. Eight years before, Pompey had made Orodes' sister march in his triumph. The daughter and the granddaughter of a Parthian king, plucked from a diplomatic marriage in Armenia, had been bit players in a show where Parthia otherwise played no part. When Surenas's day of triumph came, Paccianus was escorted by Roman lictors as Crassus himself would have been, his chariot studded with Roman skulls, his escorting carts laden with legionary eagles and erotica, his dress flapping around his knees.

Plutarch loved these stories. There was nothing like them available for his Lives of Caesar and Pompey. One of the most influential memoirs of the defeat of Crassus's army came from Cassius. Successful in his retreat to Syria, he had seen a strong need, if he were to have a political future, to show that the catastrophe had been none of his fault. Though taking over command in Syria and protecting Rome's frontier, he had to endure suspicion that scarred him for the rest of his life, humiliating jibes that he had become a date salesman from his time in the desert, hawking dried fruit to stay alive, hardly better than the man who had warned *Cave ne eas, Cave ne eas,* while Crassus's legions were leaving Brundisium. But his readers were left in no doubt of his good advice on the campaign and how it had been consistently ignored.

The Rome to which Cassius returned was different without Crassus to pull strings, buy votes, and balance the rivalry of Pompey and Caesar. When that rivalry turned to fighting, Cassius fought for Pompey. When Pompey's head was severed on a beach in Egypt, Cassius switched to serve Caesar until he led the conspirators on the Ides of March, lighting the fuse for more than another decade of civil war.

If Caesar had escaped his assassins, he would himself have invaded Parthia to bring back the lost eagles, any surviving prisoners, and maybe his former banker's head. Thanks to the dagger of Cassius, and of Crassus's supporter Trebonius, and of dozens more on the Ides of March, 44 BCE, the Parthians could, instead of fighting Caesar, trade Chinese silk, applaud Greek tragedies, squabble with one another, and expand their territories to the east. They took some of their enslaved Roman prisoners out on the road to China; their descendants were recognizable, in the border town of Merv, a century later. Orodes had Surenas executed, quietly, before prestige from such victory might produce a challenge for his throne.

Crassus's surviving son, Marcus, took due lessons from the deaths of his father and grandfather, his uncle and his brother. He played no part in Rome's civil wars, taking up public life, and then only modestly, when Caesar's adopted son was ruling Rome as the emperor Augustus. By then a return had been negotiated for Crassus's eagles, a diplomatic success that was presented on Augustus's statues as though it were a military one. There was no return for the much-abused head of Rome's first tycoon, only commemoration in a commonplace bust inside a family mausoleum.

Along the Appian Way, where Crassus had once hung the bodies of Spartacus's army, not far from the Capena Gate where he had left for Parthia, the name of the unambitious Marcus Crassus was carved on the funeral tower of Caecilia Metella, the wife who had been chosen for him for the purposes of his father's politics. It can still be seen there after two thousand years.

Chronology

All dates BCE.

Chronology

Source Notes

CHAPTER 1. THE SECRET DISRUPTER

The Lives of Crassus, Pompey, and Caesar by Plutarch (43 – ca. 119 CE) are key sources: see Plutarch, *Fall of the Roman Republic: Marius, Sulla, Crassus, Pompey, Caesar, Cicero: Six Lives,* trans. Rex Warner, rev. ed. (Harmondsworth, Eng.: Penguin, 1972); and Plutarch, *Lives,* vol. 3: *Pericles and Fabius Maximus; Nicias and Crassus,* trans. Bernadotte Perrin, Loeb Classical Library 65 (Cambridge, Mass.: Harvard University Press, 1916); Plutarch, *Lives,* vol. 5: *Agesilaus and Pompey; Pelopidas and Marcellus,* trans. Bernadotte Perrin, Loeb Classical Library 87 (Cambridge, Mass.: Harvard University Press, 1917); and Plutarch, *Lives,* vol. 7: *Demosthenes and Cicero; Alexander and Caesar,* trans. Bernadotte Perrin, Loeb Classical Library 99 (Cambridge, Mass.: Harvard University Press, 1919). The Life of Crassus is the most moralistic of the three, designed principally to preach the dangers of greed. For a modern political account, see Allen Mason Ward, *Marcus Crassus and the Late Roman Republic* (Columbia: University of Missouri Press, 1977). See also T. J. Cadoux, "Marcus Crassus: A Revaluation," *Greece & Rome* 3 (October 1956): 153–161. For Crassus's place in a broader history, see Mary Beard, *SPQR: A History of Ancient Rome* (New York: Liveright, 2015); and Mary Beard with Michael Crawford, *Rome in the Late Republic: Problems and Interpretations* (London: Duckworth, 2000); see also Theodor Mommsen, *History of Rome* (London: Everyman, 1921).

For Crassus's age, see Plutarch, *Crassus* 17.2. For Crassus's mother, see *Cicero's Letters to Atticus,* trans. D. R. Shackleton Bailey (Harmondsworth, Eng.: Penguin, 1978), 1.4.3, 12.24.2. For the fame of Crassus's wealth, see the war against Catiline in Sallust, *Catiline's War, The Jugurthine War, Histories,* ed. and trans. A. J. Woodman, rev. ed. (Harmondsworth, Eng.: Penguin, 2008), 48.5; and Tertullian's *Apologeticum* in *Apology; De Spectaculis; Minucius Felix; Octavius,* trans. T. R. Glover and Gerald H. Rendall, Loeb Classical Library 250 (Cambridge, Mass.: Harvard University Press, 1931), 11. On the trading of wealth for political power, see Cicero, *On Duties,* in *Selected Works,* trans. Michael Grant (Harmondsworth, Eng.: Penguin, 1960), 1.25.

CHAPTER 2. A FARAWAY PLACE

Knowledge of ancient Parthia is scarce, chiefly dependent on fragmented Greek and Latin sources and analysis of coinage. For a useful modern summary, see Gareth C. Sampson, *The Defeat of Rome: Crassus, Carrhae and the Invasion of the East* (reprint ed., London: Pen and Sword, 2015). For the presence of Parthians in Xerxes' army, see

Source Notes

Herodotus, *The Histories*, trans. Tom Holland (Harmondsworth, Eng.: Penguin, 2014), 7.66. For Parthians on both sides in Greek-Persian wars, see Diodorus, *Library of History*, vol. 9: *Books 18–19.65*, trans. Russel M. Geer, Loeb Classical Library 377 (Cambridge, Mass.: Harvard University Press, 1933), 18.3.3. The dynastic name Arsaces appears in Aeschylus, *Persians*, in *The Persians and Other Plays*, ed. and trans. Alan H. Sommerstein (Harmondsworth, Eng.: Penguin, 2009), 995. The claim that the Parthians originally came from Syria is in Strabo, *Geography*, vol. 5: *Books 10–12*, trans. Horace Leonard Jones, Loeb Classical Library 211 (Cambridge, Mass.: Harvard University Press, 1917), 11.9.2.

CHAPTER 3. NOTHING TO LAUGH ABOUT

Sallust, *Jugurthine War*, ed. Catalina Balmaceda and Michael Comber (Liverpool: Aris & Phillips Classical Texts, 2007), introduces the rivalry between Marius and Sulla. For the political and military impact of Marius's reforms and many other issues, there is P. A. Brunt's *The Fall of the Roman Republic and Related Essays* (Oxford: Clarendon Press, 1988). On Crassus's education, see Cicero, *Brutus; Orator,* trans. G. L. Hendrickson, H. M. Hubbell, Loeb Classical Library 342 (Cambridge: Harvard University Press, 1939), 233, 308; and Plutarch, *Crassus* 3.7. For Crassus's father's political career, see Pliny the Elder, *Natural History: A Selection*, trans. John F. Healy (London: Penguin Classics, 1991), 30.12, which relates his role in the ban on human sacrifice and controls on imported wine and perfume at 13.24, 14.95. The elder Publius Crassus is the probable authority on the tin trade referred to by Strabo in his *Geography*, vol. 3: *Books 3–5*, trans. Horace Leonard Jones, Loeb Classical Library 50 (Cambridge: Harvard University Press, 1917), 3.5.11. Plutarch describes the charges against Crassus's wife in his Life of Cicero, in *Fall of the Roman Republic* 25.4, and Crassus's escape to Spain in *Crassus* 4.1.

CHAPTER 4. INSIDE THE CAVE

For a good account of Plutarch's purposes as a biographer, see Philip A. Stadter's *Plutarch and His Roman Readers* (Oxford: Oxford University Press, 2015). E. Lo Cascio discusses the development of Roman monetary policy in "State and Coinage in the Late Republic and Early Empire," *Journal of Roman Studies* 71 (November 1981): 76–86. The story of Crassus hiding in a cave is in Plutarch, *Crassus* 4.3, 5.4, and his raising an army to leave at 6.1. Philip O. Spann, in *Quintus Sertorius and the Legacy of Sulla* (Fayetteville: University of Arkansas Press, 1987), 188, reports an attempt to identify the cave.

CHAPTER 5. CRASSUS AT WAR

The events of Crassus's lifetime recounted by the Greek official of the Roman Empire Appian (95–165 CE) are from the only surviving continuous account of the period. In *The Civil Wars,* trans. John Carter (Harmondsworth, Eng.: Penguin, 1996), he reports on Pompey and Crassus at Spoletium at 1.10.90 and on Sulla and Crassus at the Colline Gate at 1.10.93. Plutarch's accounts of the Colline Gate are at his *Crassus* 6.6 and his *Sulla* 29–30. A soldier historian writing closer to the events, Velleius Paterculus (19 BCE–31 CE), gives a florid version in *The Roman History,* trans. J. C. Yardley and Anthony A. Barrett (Indianapolis, Ind.: Hackett, 2011), 2.71.1. Plutarch describes Crassus's mission to the Marsi at *Crassus* 6.2–3 and the Tuder looting charge at 6.1.5. An excellent modern account of Sulla's tactics and ambitions is by Edward H. Bispham, "Sulla and the Populi Italici," in *L'Età di Silla,* ed. Maria Theresa Schettino and Giuseppe Zecchini (Rome: Istituto Italiano per la Storia Antica, 2018), 1–43. The most useful modern life of Pompey is Robin Seager, *Pompey the Great: A Political Biography,* 2nd ed. (Oxford: Blackwell, 2002).

CHAPTER 6. WAYS OF REVENGE

For a discussion of Roman businessmen and the *equites,* see P. A. Brunt, "The Fall of the Roman Republic," in *The Fall of the Roman Republic and Related Essays* (Oxford: Clarendon Press, 1988), 1–92. Elizabeth Rawson discusses Roman house ownership in "The Ciceronian Aristocracy and Its Properties," in *Roman Culture and Society* (Oxford: Clarendon Press, 1991), 204–222. Plutarch describes Crassus's financial gains from city fires and eventual ownership of large parts of Rome at *Crassus* 2.4. Allegations of malpractice come at *Crassus* 6.7, and his notoriety as a property developer in his Life of Cato the Younger in *Lives,* vol. 8: *Sertorius and Eumenes; Phocion and Cato the Younger,* trans. Bernadotte Perrin, Loeb Classical Library 100 (Cambridge: Harvard University Press, 1919), 19.5. For other profiteering allies of Sulla, see Cicero's first major courtroom speech, *In Defence of Sextus Roscius of Ameria,* in his *Murder Trials,* trans. Michael Grant (Harmondsworth, Eng.: Penguin, 1975), 6, 17–29. The jibe about learning to row before trying to steer is from Aristophanes' comedy *The Knights,* in *The Birds and Other Plays,* trans. David Barrett and Alan H. Sommerstein (London: Penguin, 1978), 542.

CHAPTER 7. PARTHIAN FACES

For the difficulties of using the scattered sources for Parthian history, most of them hostile, see Neilson C. Debevoise's introduction to his *Political History of Parthia* (Chicago: University of Chicago Press, 1938). See also *The Cambridge History of Iran,* vol. 3 (Cambridge: Cambridge University Press, 1983); and A. Sherwin-White, *Roman Foreign Policy in the East, 168 BC–AD 1* (London: Duckworth, 1984). For the Roman idea that trade was dishonorable, see Livy, *The War with Hannibal,* Books 21–30 of *The History of Rome from Its Foundation,* ed. Betty Radice and trans. Aubrey de Sélincourt (Harmondsworth, Eng.: Penguin, 1965), 21.63.4; and Cicero, *On Duties* 1.151.

Source Notes

CHAPTER 8. FIRE AND FINANCE

For discussion of extinguishing and profiting from street fires, see H. V. Canter, "Conflagrations in Ancient Rome," *Classical Journal* 27 (January 1932): 270–288. For the story of Timagenes, a historian hostile to Rome and once a slave of Sulla's son, see G. W. Bowersock, *Augustus and the Greek World* (Oxford: Clarendon Press, 1965). For reaction against Sulla, see Alison Rosenblitt, "The Turning Tide: The Politics of the Year 79 B.C.E.," *Transactions of the American Philological Association* 144 (Autumn 2014): 415–444. Sulla's challenge to would-be prosecutors is reported by Plutarch in *Sulla* 34.3.

CHAPTER 9. PROBLEMS WITH FOREIGNERS

A good starting point for the difficult discussion of the role of slavery in the Roman world is Keith Bradley and Paul Cartledge, eds., *The Cambridge World History of Slavery*, vol. 1: *The Ancient Mediterranean World* (Cambridge: Cambridge University Press, 2011). Cicero tells in the speech *In Defence of Aulus Cluentius Habitus* in *Murder Trials*, trans. Michael Grant (Harmondsworth, Eng.: Penguin, 1975), 111–254, of the long enslavement of a Roman, Marcus Aurius, after Rome's victory over its former Italian allies at Asculum in 89 BCE. Plutarch describes Crassus's profiting from the education and training of slaves at *Crassus* 2.5 and Julius Caesar's avoidance of being enslaved by pirates at his *Caesar* 2.3–4.

CHAPTER 10. SPARTACUS

There is an enormous modern bibliography on the insurrection of Spartacus, most of it, unsurprisingly, hostile to Crassus. Barry Strauss's *Spartacus War* (New York: Simon and Schuster, 2009) is a balanced account. I followed Spartacus's routes through Italy for *On the Spartacus Road: A Spectacular Journey Through Ancient Italy* (London: HarperPress, 2010). A useful collection of the primary sources is in Brent D. Shaw, *Spartacus and the Slave Wars: A Brief History with Documents* (New York: St. Martin's, 2001).

Appian's *Civil Wars* 14 is the primary source: the recruitment of Crassus's legions at 1.14.118, the crucifixion by Spartacus of a Roman prisoner at 1.14.119, and Crassus's eventual victory and the crucifixions of survivors along the Appian Way at 1.14.120. Crassus's brutal punishment of his own soldiers is described by Plutarch in his *Crassus* 10.3 and in Sallust, *Histories* 4.22. For the rivalry between Pompey and Crassus over the final credit for Spartacus's defeat, see Velleius Paterculus's *History* in *Compendium of Roman History; Res Gestae Divi Augusti*, trans. Frederick W. Shipley, Loeb Classical Library 152 (Cambridge: Harvard University Press, 1924), 2.30.6. For their continuing rivalry and cooperation and joint consulship, see Plutarch's *Pompey* 21.3, 22.1 and *Crassus* 7.4, 12.1, and Appian, *Civil Wars* 1.121. For the handshake of a tactical reconciliation, see Appian, *Civil Wars* 1.14.121, and Plutarch, *Pompey* 23.2. For Crassus's sensitivity about the low-level celebration of his victory, see Plutarch, *Crassus* 11.8, and Cicero's speech *Against Lucius Calpurnius Piso* in *Orations,* trans. N. H. Watts, Loeb Classical Library 252 (Cambridge: Harvard University Press, 1931), 58. Massive wealth was described by Cicero as the "sinew of war" at *Philippics* 5.5, trans. D. R. Shackleton Bailey, Loeb Classical Library 189 (Cambridge: Harvard University Press, 2009). Money was described as "coined liberty" by Fyodor Dostoyevsky in *The House of the Dead,* trans. Constance Garnett (New York: Macmillan, 1915).

CHAPTER 11. EASTERN QUESTIONS

Mary Beard begins her *SPQR* with an incisive account of the probable truths and palpable falsities of the charges against Catiline and what they mean for the study of Roman history (*SPQR: A History of Ancient Rome* [New York: Liveright, 2015]). Crassus's role in disrupting trials and pulling political strings seems as firmly established as it is hard to pin down. Sallust's version, with its anxieties about the moral decline of Rome, has the simultaneous aim of protecting Julius Caesar. Crassus tries to warn Catiline in Sallust's account, in *Catiline's War* 48.3–4, and uses his house for the conspirator's house arrest at 47.3–4. Crassus is accused by Velleius Paterculus of disrupting the trial of Pompey's ally Manilius in his *History* 2.3.4. Cicero describes Crassus's helping him to buy a house in *Letters to Friends,* trans. D. R. Shackleton Bailey, 3 vols., Loeb Classical Library 205, 216, and 230 (Cambridge: Harvard University Press, 2001), 5.6.2, and Crassus's fears of Pompey's cooperation with the Senate at 5.7.1. Crassus's proposal that Rome make Egypt a province is described by Plutarch in *Crassus* 13.1.

CHAPTER 12. THE NATURE OF MONEY

The best account of Clodius and the Bona Dea scandal is by W. Jeffrey Tatum in *The Patrician Tribune: Publius Clodius Pulcher* (Chapel Hill: University of North Carolina Press, 2010). Plutarch describes Crassus's backing Caesar's campaign to be Pontifex Maximus at *Caesar* 7.1–2 and his leaving Rome for Asia at *Pompey* 43.1. The story of the Tolosa treasure from Delphi is told by Strabo, *Geography* 4.1.13. For Pompey's extraordinary triumph, see Mary Beard's *Roman Triumph* (Cambridge: Belknap Press of Harvard University Press, 2007).

CHAPTER 13. A THREE-HEADED MONSTER

Horace, *Odes* 2.1, in *The Complete Odes and Epodes,* trans. W. G. Shepherd (London: Penguin, 1983), fixes 60 BCE as the turning point for the Roman Republic. The description of Crassus, Pompey, and Caesar as a three-headed monster was by Marcus Terentius Varro and comes from Appian, *Civil Wars* 4.2.9. The Ravenna and Luca conferences are reported by Plutarch at *Caesar* 21 and at *Crassus* 14.5. Luca is also reported by Appian, *Civil Wars* 2.3.17. The verdict on its outcome is given by Velleius

Source Notes

Paterculus, *History* 2.46.1; by Plutarch, *Crassus* 14.5–6; and by Appian, *Civil Wars* 2.3.17. Cassius Dio (ca. 163 – ca. 235 CE) describes, in his *Roman History: The Reign of Augustus,* trans. Ian Scott-Kilvert (Harmondsworth, Eng.: Penguin, 1987), 39.28.1–5, the Senate mourning for Rome's lost freedom. The best modern account of Cassius Dio, who after Plutarch is the second main source for the last part of Crassus's life, is by Fergus Millar, *A Study of Cassius Dio* (Oxford: Oxford University Press, 1964).

Cassius Dio describes the role of Crassus's son Publius in Gaul at *Roman History* 39.46. Caesar gives his own account at *Gallic War* 2.2.4, 3.1.2, 8.2. *The Landmark Julius Caesar: The Complete Works,* ed. and trans. Kurt A. Raaflaub (New York: Pantheon, 2017), is an excellent translation and commentary. Cicero praises Publius at *Letters to Friends* 13.16 and notes his excess ambition at *Brutus* 28. On the uncertain question of the ages of Crassus's two sons, see Ronald Syme, "The Sons of Crassus," *Latomus* 39 (1980): 403–408, reprinted in Anthony R. Birley, ed., *Roman Papers,* vol. 3 (Oxford: Clarendon Press, 1984).

CHAPTER 14. HOW TO BE FIRST

Popular opposition to the Parthian war is noted by Plutarch, *Crassus* 16.3, and by Appian, *Civil Wars* 2.3.18. Plutarch's account of the argument whether Crassus was legally able to start war against Parthia if he chose is at *Crassus* 13.5 and *Pompey* 52.3. For Crassus back among the Marsi, see Pliny, *Natural History* 2.147, and Horace, *Odes* 3.5.10. Cicero relates the warning to Crassus from the fig seller at *On Divination,* in *On Old Age; On Friendship; On Divination,* trans. W. A. Falconer, Loeb Classical Library 154 (Cambridge: Harvard University Press, 1923), 2.84, his last meal with Crassus at *Letters to Friends* 1.9.20, and the attempts at Rome to curtail Crassus's powers at *Letters to Friends* 5.8.1. For other issues in Crassus's departure for Parthia, see Adelaide D. Simpson, "The Departure of Crassus for Parthia," *Transactions and Proceedings of the American Philological Association* 69 (1938): 532–541.

CHAPTER 15. A DIVINE BULL'S WARNING

For the Roman sense of superiority to other peoples, the best account is J. P. V. D. Balsdon, *Romans and Aliens* (London: Duckworth, 1979). The essential glories of Italy are described by Cicero in *The Speech Concerning the Response of the Soothsayers* in *Orations,* trans. N. H. Watts, Loeb Classical Library 158 (Cambridge: Harvard University Press, 1923), 19, and in Pliny, *Natural History* 37.202. The warning from Deiotarus is reported by Plutarch at *Crassus* 17.1–2. The first campaign is outlined at Plutarch, *Crassus* 17.4, also at Cassius Dio, *Roman History* 40.13.4. The best historical overview of the whole region is Peter Green, *Alexander to Actium* (London: Thames and Hudson, 1994).

Source Notes

CHAPTER 16. HAIRS ON A MAN'S PALM

Several possible early accounts of the road to Carrhae are known about but lost. Nicolas of Damascus (ca. 64 BCE–ca. 1 CE) wrote 144 books of history from the court of Herod the Great. Publius Crassus had a former slave called Apollonius who may have described what he saw. Quintus Dellius is often thought to be a prime source for Plutarch's moral warnings. So, too, Gaius Cassius himself.

The warning from Vagises is reported by Plutarch at *Crassus* 18.2. For the interpretation of it as a sexual insult, see Gilles Courtiou, "Vagises' Virtuous Hand: An Unforeseen Note on Plutarch, *Life of Crassus* 18, 3," *Iranian Studies* 51 (2018): 633–642.

CHAPTER 17. CAMELS AND BOWS

Cassius Dio's account differs from that of Plutarch principally in its view that Crassus was betrayed by treacherous local advice. My account of the battle largely follows that of Plutarch. Surenas is introduced at *Crassus* 21.6–7. Publius's breakout from the main force is at *Crassus* 25.2, the return of his head on a spear at 26.4.5.

CHAPTER 18. A BRAWL OVER A HORSE

Crassus's speech after Publius's death is reported by Plutarch at *Crassus* 26.5.6 and his decision to abandon the wounded at *Crassus* 27.5.6.

CHAPTER 19. CRASSUS'S TRIUMPH

Cassius Dio tells the story of Crassus's head filled with gold in his *Roman History* 40.27.3. The historian Lucius Annaeus Florus (ca. 74–130 CE) includes it in his *Epitome of Roman History,* trans. E. S. Forster, Loeb Classical Library 231 (Cambridge: Harvard University Press, 1929), 1.46.10. The story of Crassus's head used onstage comes from Plutarch at *Crassus* 33.3 and is discussed by David Braund, "Dionysiac Tragedy in Plutarch, *Crassus,*" *Classical Quarterly* 43 (December 1993): 368–374.

Acknowledgments

Thanks to all who read the text and talked to me about Crassus: to Mary Beard, Heather Gold, Susan Laity, Caroline Michel, James Romm, Ruth Scurr, Andrew Sillett, Paul Webb. *Lectores optimi,* the very best of readers.

Index

Index

Index

Index

Index

Index